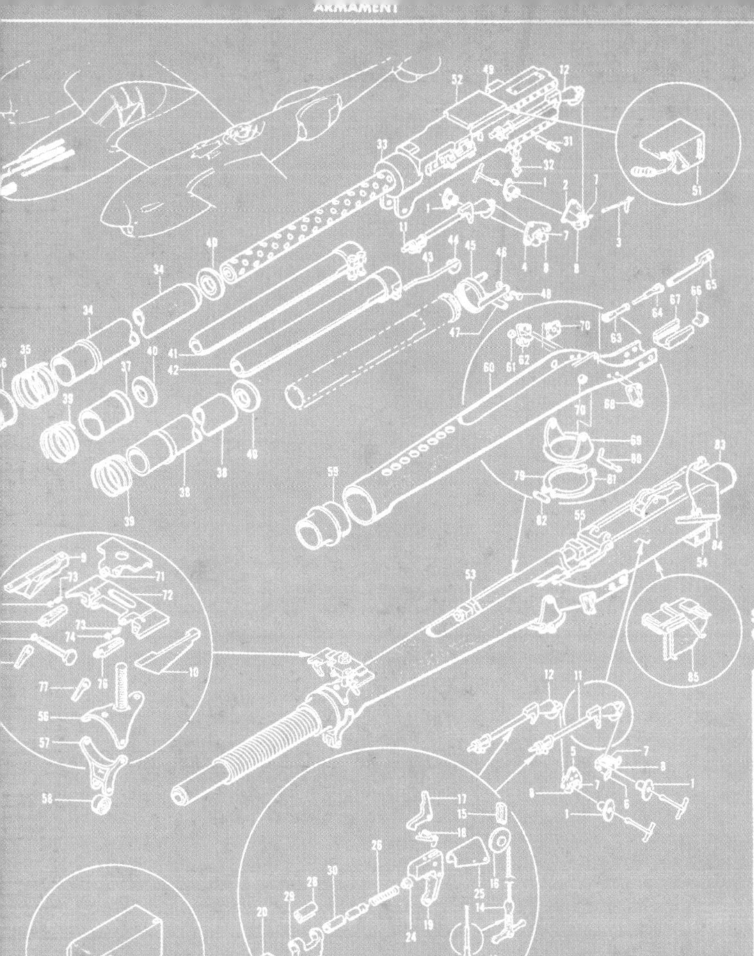

Fig. 46 — Armament And Fittings And Camera

RESTRICTED

NAMES: Upper ... ret—upper local control
Sperry ... er gun turret—Sperry
Deck t...

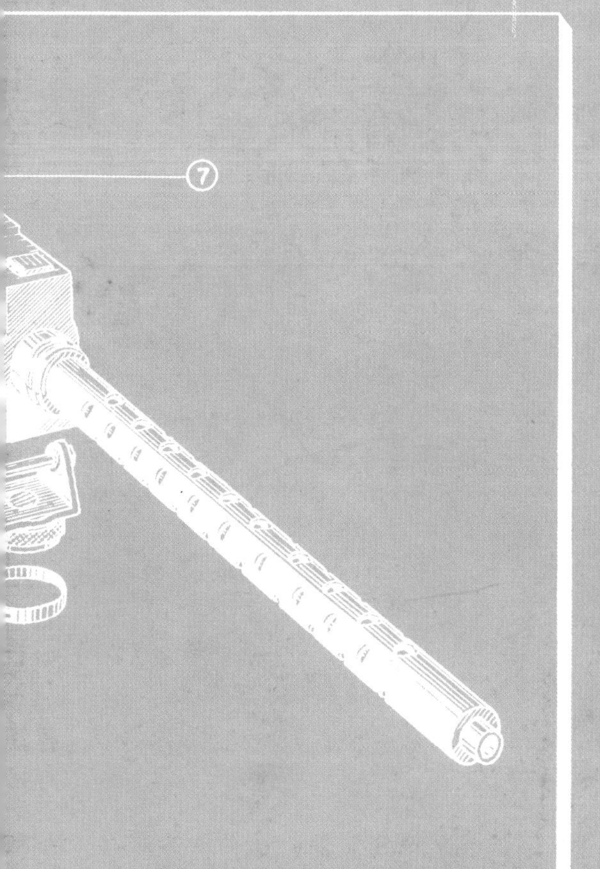

Section II
Group Assembly Parts List

RESTRICTED
AN 01-75-4A
ARMAMENT

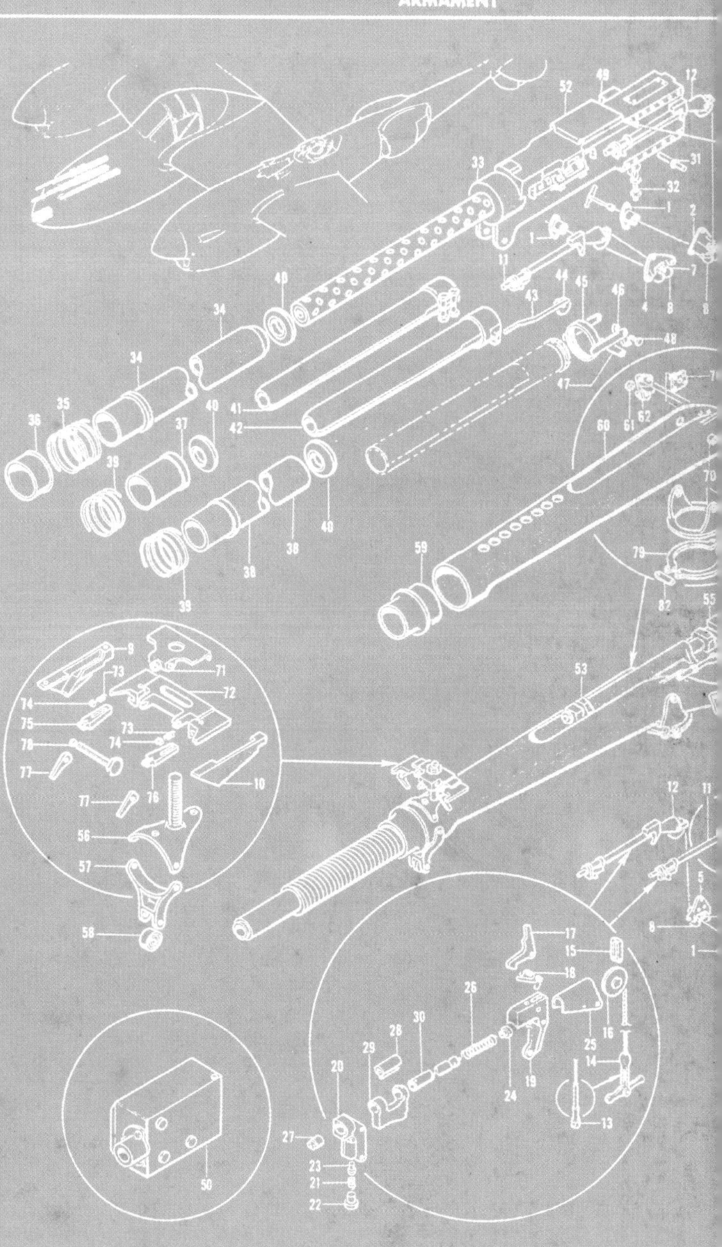

Fig. 46 — Armament And Fittings And Camera

RESTRICTED

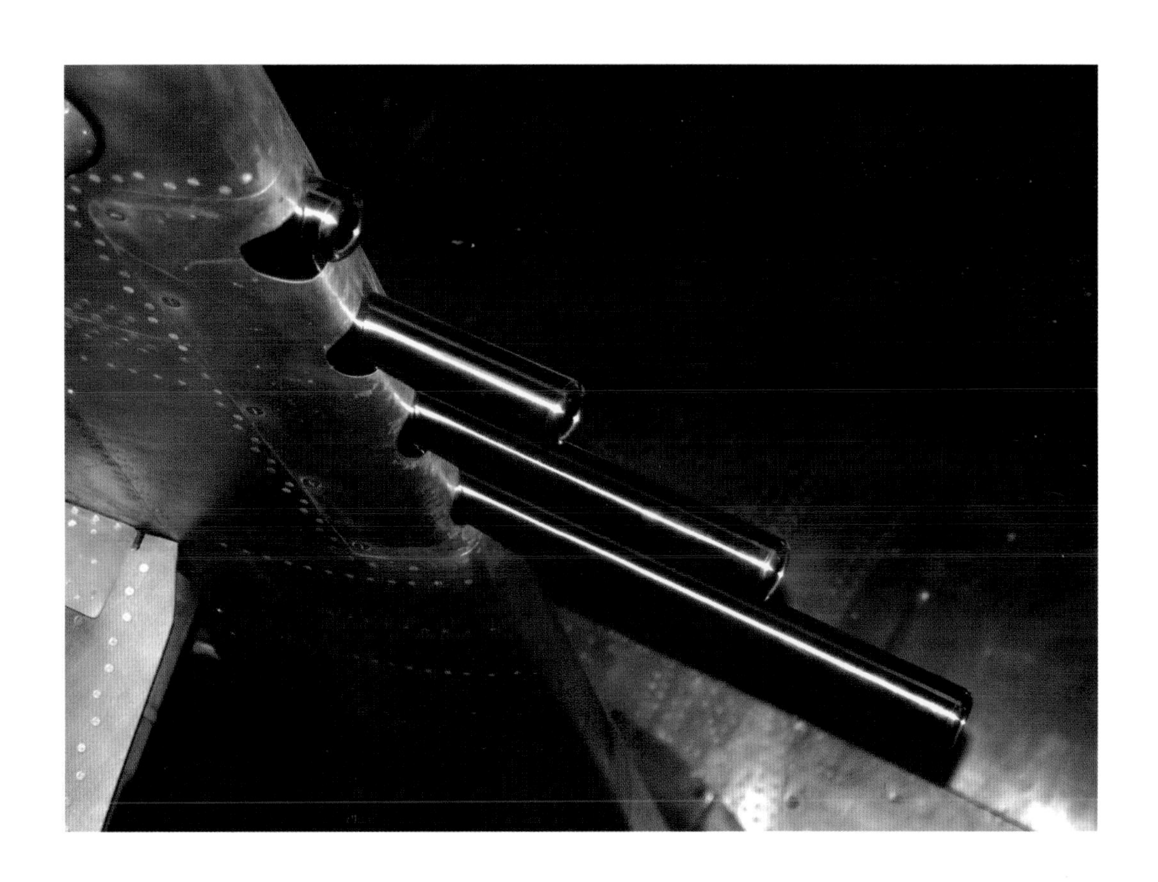

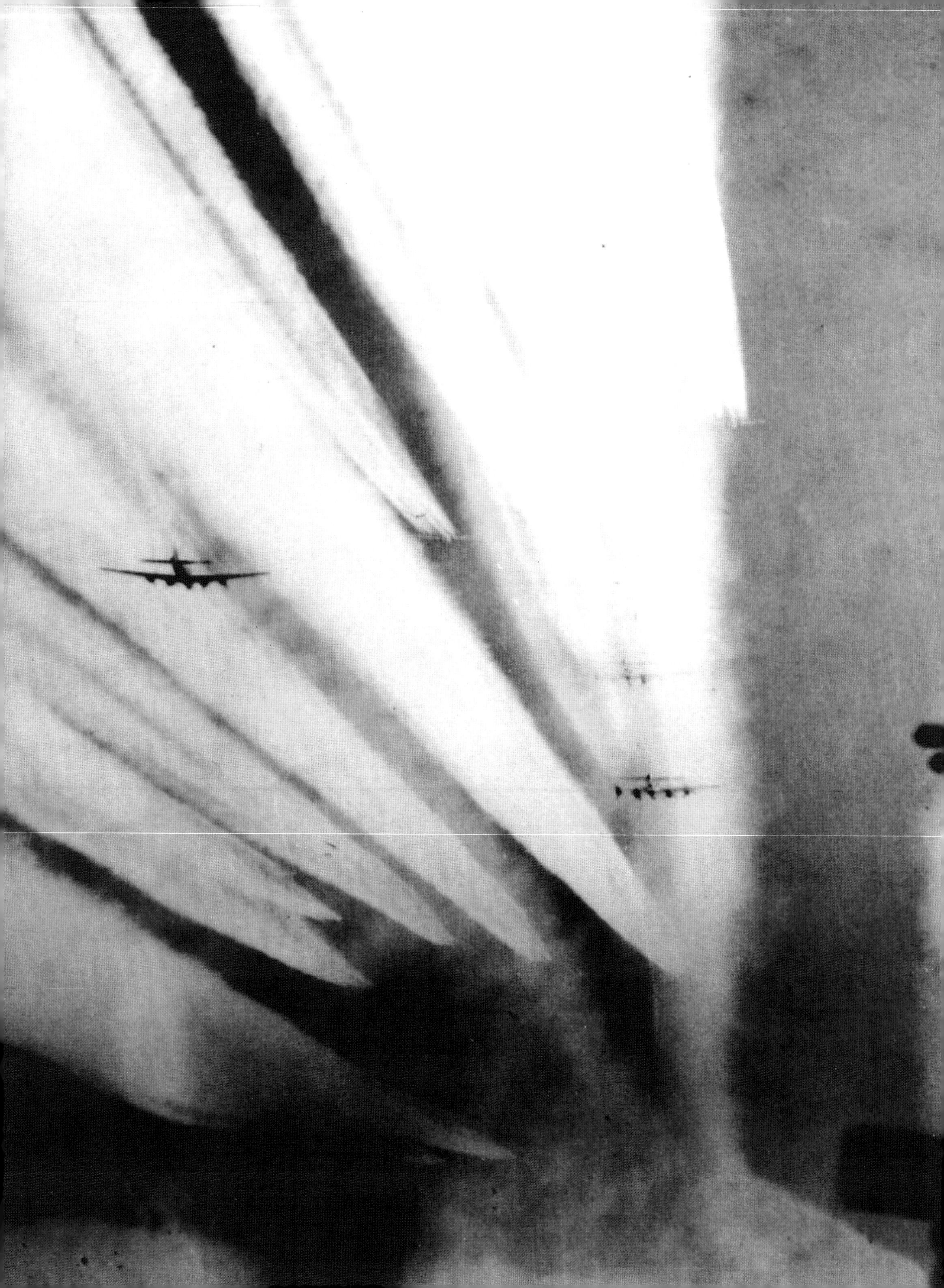

WEAPONS of the Eighth Air Force

FREDERICK A. JOHNSEN

MBI

First published in 2003 by MBI Publishing Company, Galtier Plaza, Suite 200, 380 Jackson Street, St. Paul, MN 55101-3885 USA

MBI Publishing Company books are also available at discounts in bulk quantity for industrial or sales-promotional use. For details write to Special Sales Manager at Motorbooks International Wholesalers & Distributors Galtier Plaza, Suite 200, 380 Jackson Street, St. Paul, MN 55101-3885 USA

Library of Congress Cataloging-in-Publication Data

Johnsen, Frederick A.
Weapons of the Eighth Air Force / by Frederick A. Johnsen.
p. cm.
ISBN 0-7603-1340-7 (hc. : alk. paper)
1. Airplanes, Military—United States—History—20th century. 2. World War, 1939-1945—Aerial operations, American. 3. World War, 1939-1945—Campaigns—Europe. 4. United States. Army Air Forces. Air Force, 8th. I. Title.

UG1243.J64 2003
940.54'4973—dc21

On the front cover: Eighth Air Force B-17 formations were more than mirages over Texas decades after the war ended. Pioneers in the appreciation of World War II aircraft, the Confederate Air Force (CAF) created dramatic scenes of mock air battles every October over Harlingen, Texas. During the 1977 Air Show, the CAF's first B-17G, *Texas Raiders,* raised its right wing to turn with the silver B-17G *Class of '44,* later renamed *Sentimental Journey* by the organization's Arizona Wing. *Author photo*

On the back cover: (A-19) The high squadron is in contrail-producing conditions in this 1st Bomb Division B-17 formation. Frequent cloud cover above Germany necessitated rapid development and deployment of bombing radar to enable Eighth Air Force to keep up its campaign of precision bombing. *Malcolm Gougon collection, Flight Test Historical Museum* **(6-8)** It was a beautiful day for flying above patchy clouds when *TIKA-IV* of the 361st Fighter Group was photographed in color. Exhaust constituents have deposited a visible layer over part of the fuselage national insignia. The pilot grinned from his perch near six victory marks painted just below the canopy. *AAF* **(2-26)** Twenty-year-old Staff Sergeant Robert L. Taylor posed in an Eighth Air Force B-17 waist section littered with empty .50-caliber brass shell casings. The wooden ammunition crate on the floor behind Taylor suggests this was a staged photo to depict combat conditions. The heavy flak apron provided some lateral protection to the gunner. *AAF/NARA*

On the frontispiece: Art and symmetry can be found even in the destructive power of four wing-mounted machine guns in a P-47M Thunderbolt at the Yanks Air Museum, Chino, California. Smooth-jacketed guns are staggered to facilitate ammunition feeding. *Author's collection*

On the title page: Contrails issuing from these B-17s were a highway marker dreaded by bomber crews. The white plumes led surely to the aircraft that caused them, and pointed out their presence to friend and foe alike. Eighth Air Force crews tried to optimize en-route altitudes to avoid climatic conditions that could result in the production of contrails. *USAFA/Brown collection*

Edited by Steve Gansen
Designed by Rochelle Schultz

Printed in China

Contents

Foreword

The era of the Eighth Air Force in World War II stands as the only testimony to theories of protracted bombardment campaigns and thousand-plane raids. As quickly as the force to fight Germany was conjured up beginning in 1942, it faded after 1945 behind newer weapons and strategies in the Cold War.

Bombers bristling with machine guns at every quarter, engaged by fighter swarms in running gun battles, gave way after the war to operations intended to either mask the presence of offensive aircraft or sweep the skies of opposition before calling the big bombers in. In darker Cold War scenarios, bomber survival was not a given.

With the Eighth Air Force, planners had essentially two weapons: iron gravity bombs and .50-caliber machine guns. These were housed in a variety of aircraft and operated by Americans from all walks of life in a campaign that lasted less than three years, which felt like a lifetime for those fighting in the skies. In that time, the campaigns and the aircraft of the Eighth Air Force were not static. Experience dictated changes in tactics and the rapid evolution of newer and better turrets, gun sights, and escort fighters.

There was a not-so-secret weapon of the Eighth Air Force as well: the human element. The bravery exhibited by young Americans going into battle high over Europe was admired by our allies even though they grimaced at the American haughtiness that presumed daylight precision bombing could be undertaken no matter what the obstacles were.

And then, in a flash, the Eighth's era was over. The primary strategic weapons of the campaign, the B-17 and B-24 heavy bombers, never again served in that role for the U.S. Air Force in future conflicts. The dawning jet age relegated the piston-powered fighters of the wartime Eighth to ancillary duties for a few waning years. When, in the 1950s, Cold War B-36s were lightened by removing everything but the tail guns, what was already known about the future of air attacks became even clearer: future air wars would demand air superiority or else high attrition would come at the hands of more capable fighters. There would be no more gunners trading volleys with fighters over long stretches of sky. By the time B-52s joined B-1Bs and B-2s over Iraq in 2003, none of the bombers carried a gun and all those onboard survived.

If the story of the Eighth Air Force and its weapons is an anachronism unique to the 1940s, it is also as important to the evolution of civilization as the rise and fall of knights and the age of sail. This volume explores those aerial weapons that blossomed and then disappeared quickly, but it does so with the respectful acknowledgment that the skills and bravery that people brought to these weapons was and is an asset far greater than the machines themselves. Americans of any era can ask for no better role models.

Author Fred Johnsen has turned a penchant for heavy bombers into a timeless digest of the weapons of the Eighth Air Force in World War II. With photos from many holdings, his narrative adds to our understanding of the mighty Eighth and of the people who manned those weapons in pursuit of freedom.

—Richard P. Hallion, Ph.D., former chief historian
United States Air Force

Artist's Note

When I got the call from the publisher to do the full-color profile illustrations for *Weapons of the Eighth Air Force*, the adrenaline immediately started pumping. I have loved drawing and painting airplanes since I was a kid in grade school, and the feeling has never changed.

After determining which profiles to feature, I was off and running, getting as much accurate information as possible on these very colorful airplanes. Research was not a problem. With few exceptions I have seen most of them many times over the years as an aviation artist, but I wanted to get a good variety of types and paint schemes that would show the reader what these planes really looked like. I think they typify the best and most colorful in the Eighth Air Force inventory.

Of course, the personal nose art on some of these planes was the most fun of all. Named after moms and dads, comic book characters, monsters, and pin-up girls, these names often reflected the historical fabric of America at the time, and I was very careful to get the authentic look of these hand-painted decorations that meant so much to their air crews.

All in all, it was great fun. I hope a good portion of the book's readers are new to these wonderful, now old, airplanes and will come to appreciate their historical significance like so many others before them.

—Sonny Schug

Preface

When the Eighth Air Force rushed headlong and deliberately into German-held skies over Europe in 1942, it was with a stereotypically American chemistry of self-assurance, bravado, stoicism, and—no doubt—healthy fear masked by humor. Allied protocols gave priority to prosecution of the European war while placing Japan second in line, which only heightened the sense of urgency the airmen of the new Eighth Air Force felt.

The Eighth Air Force was the standard bearer of American airpower theory, a bold concept forged in turmoil, and sometimes in defiance, during peacetime. Centered on the concept of high-altitude strategic daylight bombardment, American airpower called for equal doses of skill and courage. Another element of the American arsenal was a vast and ever-expanding production capacity in the virtually inviolate boundaries of the United States. This ability to produce and modify warplanes on a grand scale gave the fliers of the Eighth Air Force a variety of weapons in their fight against Germany.

The aircraft of the Eighth Air Force had their own foibles. No amount of positive public relations spin could kept a vaunted B-17 aloft if flak ripped it open like a feather pillow, spewing its contents into the rarified atmosphere at 25,000 feet. If the long-ranging B-24s suffered from the added weight of bolt-on armor plating the crews didn't seem to mind. Even the rakish P-51 Mustang, the ultimate escort fighter, harbored a deadly trait: pilots were told never to ditch the Mustang in water, because its large belly air scoop dug in viciously, often with fatal results.

This volume looks at the machines of the Eighth Air Force in many of their iterations. But those machines would not have evolved and won a war without brave and innovative men in their cockpits and skilled men and women building them back in the United States. As this book is a commemoration of the machines of the Eighth Air Force in World War II, let it also be a tribute to the men and women of that heroic era. Every day, we run out of time to say "thank you" to more and more veterans of that time. It is hoped that this book will convey that deep sense of appreciation, while perpetuating the memory of those who risked everything and those who have passed on. Even as the finishing touches were being applied to this volume, taps and a 21-gun salute paid tribute to the passing of World War II veteran and aviation historian Peter M. Bowers. There's a lot of Pete's mentoring and stewardship in this book, and this volume is respectfully dedicated to his memory.

The study of World War II airpower is a constantly renewing challenge. More than a half-century after the end of the war, the volume of documentation produced by the U.S. Army Air Forces between 1941 and 1945 still masks some nuggets of information like the mountains of the 19th-century Comstock Lode still hide silver and gold. Hopefully, this book will reinforce some cherished notions about the aircraft of the Eighth Air Force while retiring once and for all some myths that have been around far too long, and, I expect, future explorations into this field will further refine our knowledge and understanding of what went on in the skies over Europe from 1942 to 1945.

Many people and organizations deserve mention for their contributions to my understanding of the Eighth Air Force and its machines. My special thanks go to the staff of the Air Force Historical Research Agency, a tremendous archive of official papers. Other noteworthy

The bright red rudder cap identifies this B-17G as part of the 490th Bomb Group. It is returning to its base in Eye, England. USAFA/Brown

collections include the Air Force Academy Special Collections, the National Archives, the Eighth Air Force Museum at Barksdale Air Force Base, and the San Diego Aerospace Museum.

Individuals lending the benefit of their experience and expertise include Peter M. Bowers, Jerry Cole, Archie Difante, Richard P. Hallion, Ben Howser, Don Keller, Jim Kiernan and Sharon D. Vance Kiernan, Jeffrey L. Kolln, Al Loyd, Duane Reed (U.S. Air Force Academy), Carl Scholl, Bob Sturges, and Ray Wagner. The men and women of the 91st Bomb Group Memorial Association were most hospitable and helpful at their reunion in Tacoma, Washington, in September 2002.

Attribution is essential to good history and good journalism. The text and photo selection are my responsibility, and I have endeavored to make them as accurate as possible. A check of my source documents listed in this book will help reveal my thought process.

Abbreviations in some captions and footnote citations include: AAF (Army Air Forces), AFHRA (Air Force Historical Research Agency), NARA (National Archives and Records Administration), SDAM (San Diego Aerospace Museum), USAF (United States Air Force), and USAFA (United States Air Force Academy).

In this volume, numbered air forces are spelled out (Eighth Air Force; Ninth Air Force) and groups and squadrons are listed with numerals (92nd Bomb Group; 1st Fighter Group).

Descriptions of various aircraft in this book include references to block numbers. These were production identifiers within specific models. A P-38F, for example, was further categorized by its block number and factory identifier. A P-38F-15-LO was a Block-15 F-model, which introduced features including maneuvering flap settings. LO indicated its factory of origin, Lockheed Burbank, in California. A B-17G-50-DL was a Block 50 G-model Fortress built under contract by Douglas at Long Beach, hence the identifier DL.

And now please conjure with me a runway nudged into green British farm fields. The damp silence is broken, and then obliterated, by the roar of hundreds of radial engines as B-24s waddle, nose to tail, toward the beginning of the runway. They bob as brakes are applied, then shudder visibly as all four engines are brought up to power for last-minute performance checks before brake release starts a tortuous run along the pavement. To the initiate, the lumbering Liberator seems sluggish, incapable of breaking ground. To the pilots aged in their 20s, seasoned first in training and now in the Big League, as pundits call the European Theater, the B-24 is coming to life as it always does. It inevitably metamorphoses from a hulking kind of livestock on the ground to an almost gracious bird in flight, its slender wings able to flex up more than a foot at the tips. Zephyrs of wind swirl around inside the fuselage, and the machine seems to creak a bit as it hits prop wash from bombers ahead of it. But it's all in a mission for a bomber crew of the Eighth Air Force. Ahead are the treacheries of high-altitude flight: frostbite and oxygen-deprivation for the unwary. Ahead are flak gunners and fighter pilots intent on making this mission an impossible hell of attrition. But why dwell on that now, as verdant England rolls beneath the wings? The job has to be done, and the crews of the Eighth Air Force said they'd do it.

CHAPTER 1

Shaping a Force to Fight Germany

Early 97th Bomb Group B-17Es sometimes carried British camouflage colors consisting of Dark Green and Dark Earth, and upper surfaces that met in a wavy line with Deep Sky Blue undersurfaces. The aging British paints were still visible when Generals Eisenhower and Spaatz reviewed enlisted men at attention in front of *Yankee Doodle* in England. At this point, it no longer flew in combat. *Yankee Doodle* carried General Ira Eaker, then commander of VIII Bomber Command, on the Eighth Air Force's inaugural heavy bombardment mission from England over Rouen, France, on August 17, 1942. AAF photo via Erwin Steele, 91st Bomb Group

An incongruously luxurious staff car in flat olive-drab paint heralds the arrival of General Carl A. Spaatz (hands in pockets) and General Dwight D. Eisenhower (hands on hips) to view the veteran B-17E *Yankee Doodle*, serial number 41-9023. By the time the photo was taken, a slick B-17F Plexiglas nose had replaced the shorter metal-ribbed cage originally attached to E-model Fortresses. A number of surviving Eighth Air Force B-17Es plied the skies in noncombat duties once newer models replaced them. AAF photo via Erwin Steele, 91st Bomb Group

Between the first B-17E sorties of August 1942 to the last heavy bomber activity in May 1945, 5,548 Fortresses and Liberators were lost on combat missions in the European Theater of Operations (ETO). Of those, the number downed by Axis fighters (2,452) was virtually the same as the number lost to antiaircraft fire (2,439). Another 657 heavy bombers on ETO combat missions were lost due to other causes.[1]

If those numbers were inconsistent with recent air campaigns where the loss of even a single aircraft makes national headlines, the Eighth Air Force in World War II operated under different constraints in a different time. The air war over Europe was the archetype of a strategic bombing campaign. Bombing efforts in World War I had only hinted at the capabilities of the air weapon; earnest proponents of airpower did their best to make strategic bombardment a decisive tool from 1942 to 1945.

With but few experimental exceptions, the bombing of Fortress Europe was accomplished with unguided bombs. Blunt, box-finned steel casings filled with high explosives rained down on Europe in a series of campaigns. From 25,000 feet, a stick of gravity bombs could stray hundreds of feet or more from the aim point, with accuracy hindered further by imperfections as slight as frozen mud on the surfaces of the bombs. Eighth Air Force B-17s and B-24s took hundreds of tons of free-falling bombs to temporarily knock out a single V-1 launch site in 1944; one satellite guided smart bomb could to better today.

A gaggle of B-17Fs shows Eighth Air Force markings in transition in the summer of 1943. That June, U.S. national insignia were modified by the addition of white rectangular bars on the sides of the blue disk containing the star; in the same month, Eighth Air Force assigned geometric designs with bomb group letters to its heavy bomber forces. In the photo, the top B-17F appears to carry the letter G of the 385th Bomb Group in a white square on the vertical fin; the lowest Fort has not received a group letter, and all three B-17s still have the 1942-style insignia with no bars. Jeffrey L. Kolln collection

The story of the Eighth Air Force is one of optimism and determination in the face of withering enemy fire, skepticism even among friends, and an impersonal priority list for the Allied cause that did not always mesh with Eighth Air Force's own agenda. Especially in the early war years, before American industrial capacity was largely converted from peacetime production to the creation of combat materiel, the Allies felt compelled to parcel out more resources against Germany than Japan. Germany was clearly seen as the most worrisome foe. Against that backdrop, the Eighth Air Force was poised to become the best-equipped and most-watched entity in the Army Air Forces (AAF).

There's a genealogical quirk in the lineage of Eighth Air Force brought about by wartime reorganization of forces in Europe. Eighth Air Force was constituted and activated in January 1942 in the United States. At about the same time, one of its key components, VIII Bomber Command, was activated at Langley Field, Virginia, on February 1, 1942. Within two weeks, that command had relocated to Savannah, Georgia. On February 23, 1942, the command was moved to England before the Eighth Air Force arrived overseas, and it remained there until the war in Europe ended in May 1945. Units began arriving in England in the spring of 1942; then on August 17, Boeing B-17E Flying Fortresses inaugurated America's heavy bombardment campaign against German-held targets on the Continent.[2]

VIII Bomber Command prosecuted the war of strategic bombardment in the European Theater of Operations as part of Eighth Air Force until February 22, 1944, when Eighth Air Force was redesignated U.S. Strategic Air Forces in Europe (USSTAF), with increased overall responsibilities that encompassed aspects of Eighth, Ninth, and Fifteenth

Smoke obscures Münster, Germany, as B-17Fs pay a call on October 10, 1943. A wartime censor has cut data, probably including identity of the bomb group, from the legend at the bottom of the photo. Bob Sturges collection

Ever grim in countenance, Curtis LeMay commanded Eighth Air Force's 305th Bomb Group until mid-1943, when he took over the 4th Bombardment Wing, followed by 3rd Bombardment Division later that year. LeMay is credited with innovating tight formation boxes that maximized defense against fighters, and with pioneering the lead bombardier concept, in which bombers in a formation released their loads on cue from a highly qualified bombardier in the lead plane. USAFA/Brown collection

Air Forces in the ongoing fight against Germany. To fill the numbered air force void when Eighth Air Force became USSTAF, the veteran VIII Bomber Command was redesignated Eighth Air Force that same day.[3]

By July 16, 1945, two months after the end of the European war, the Eighth Air Force moved in name only, without personnel or airplanes, to Okinawa, intending to help finish the Pacific war. Now the mighty Eighth, whose early priorities in Europe had presumably caused the Pacific timetable to be slowed, was arriving to accelerate the demise of Japan's war-making capability. But even as some personnel and units were being assigned before the Pacific war ended, Eighth Air Force combat against Japan was not to be; Japan stopped fighting the month after Eighth Air Force came to Okinawa. The mighty Eighth's signature wartime accomplishment remained the vaulting of Germany's so-called Atlantic Wall.

The Eighth Air Force's official list of wartime commanders is actually the roster of VIII Bomber Command leaders up to February 22, 1944, and includes some of the most famous names in strategic bombardment: Major General Ira C. Eaker took charge on February 23, 1942, followed by Brigadier General Newton Longfellow on December 2 of that year. Major General Frederick L. Anderson assumed command of Eighth Air Force on July 1, 1943, succeeded by world-famous Lieutenant General James H. Doolittle on January 6, 1944. Major General William E. Kepner assumed command May 10, 1945, with General Doolittle returning to command the organization on July 19, 1945, a scant three days after the Eighth was established on Okinawa.[4]

Similarly, the USSTAF list of commanders as traced by Air Force lineage and honors specialists reads like the

Blind Date, **a B-17F-90-BO of the 388th Bomb Group's 560th Bomb Squadron, earns another mission bomb symbol from gunner Sgt. Palvin M. Lukken. The heavily ribbed and protruding cheek-gun window used a cylindrical K-5 gun mount to provide a better forward field of fire than earlier B-17 cheek guns. However, the ultimate answer to B-17 forward fire-power requirements was the chin turret installed on G-model Fortresses.** AAF photo

One of the most often repeated nicknames of England-based B-17s, *Piccadilly Lily* was later immortalized in the book and motion picture, *Twelve O' Clock High.* This B-17F carries the Eighth Air Forces common nose gun modification in a depression in the upper part of the Plexiglas. Note the placement of the cheek-gun window, in the middle of three windows and on the right side of the nose on some Lockheed-Vega F-models. A typical B-17F cheek-window arrangement had the enlarged gun window forward on the right side and in the center on the left side. USAFA/Brown collection

roster of Eighth Air Force commanders up to February 22, 1944. Names of commanders who served as the leader of the Eighth Air Force before the designation shuffle were: Brigadier General Asa N. Duncan, as of January 28, 1942, until succeeded by Major General Carl Spaatz on May 5, 1942. Lieutenant General Ira C. Eaker assumed command on December 1, 1942, until succeeded by General Spaatz on January 6, 1944, who continued as USSTAF commander until the end of the war in Europe.[5] If the change of commanders and the shuffling of titles between Eighth Air Force, VIII Bomber Command, and USSTAF looks confusing in retrospect, one constant remains: from August 17, 1942, until May 1945, heavy bomber crews abetted by fighter pilots under an organization designated as the Eighth Air Force carried the war to Germany.

Simply amassing men and machines in England for a war with Germany was insufficient; for a variety of reasons, Eighth Air Force needed specific marching orders to conduct war against Germany. While AAF leaders wanted to husband the air weapon as a distinct fighting force not to be overly entangled with the operations of ground armies, the Air Force could not operate in a vacuum. The needs of other armed services, even of entire nations like England and the Soviet Union, would be addressed by specific Eighth Air Force actions before the war was through.

In 1942 there was pressure to launch AAF bombing missions over the Continent from England, in part as a morale boost and a show of presence by the newly arrived Americans. A Fourth of July coastal sweep by twin-engine Douglas Boston attack bombers was the first official foray by American bomber crews out of England. The AAF's 15th Bombardment Squadron (Light) was assigned to VIII Bomber Command between May 14 and September 14, 1942, and it was men of this squadron flying

Right: On a cobblestone quay glistening with rain, a crane hoists an American bomb destined for a German target. An ongoing logistics effort was required to keep a steady stream of bombs raining down on Axis targets. This effort involved moving bombs across the Atlantic, delivering them into port cities in the United Kingdom, and trans-shipping them by rail to the Eighth Air Force bomb dumps. AAF

A chaplain met with the kneeling crew of the Eighth Air Force B-17G *Fifinella,* ostensibly just before a mission, although the cheek gun visible in the photo does not have its removable barrel assembly in place. Fortunately, numerous photos of Eighth Air Force activities were made on Kodachrome color transparency film, a color-stable film that has survived the decades even while other vintage color films have faded and deteriorated. AAF photo

twin-engine attack bombers who first bombed the Continent as part of the VIII structure, not the heavy bombers that would become the Eighth Air Force's signature.[6] Several days before this raid, Captain Charles C. Kegelman, commander of the 15th Squadron, became the first Eighth Air Force airman to bomb enemy-held Europe when he participated in a mission with a dozen Royal Air Force Douglas Boston bombers on June 29.[7]

Even though the Allies agreed on a Europe-first combat priority, that decision encompassed a lot of geography and two major theaters of operations, the European and Mediterranean. As Eighth Air Force began sending aircraft and men to England in 1942 to create its vision of a strategic bombardment force, its timetable was quickly challenged by the need for AAF units to support Allied efforts in North Africa. These demands led to the creation of Twelfth Air Force, which siphoned off some of Eighth Air Force's assets. This was followed by extended temporary tours by some of Eighth Air Force's early B-24 Liberator groups to North Africa in the summer of 1943 to bomb oil fields in Ploesti, Romania. At the same time, the Soviet Union was urging the opening of a second fighting front against the Germans to relieve pressure on the Soviets. Since Western Europe was not yet ripe for an Allied invasion, this front had to come in the Mediterranean, out of the Eighth Air Force's territory. In fact, Eighth Air Force planners argued their war launched from England should be considered a second front in its own right, but assets were nonetheless cleaved off for the Mediterranean. Overlapping these diversions of Eighth Air Force men and machines was the sobering realization that unescorted daylight missions over heavily defended German targets weren't as feasible as pre-war planners had thought they would be. The lack of long-range escort fighters hobbled Eighth's reach in 1942 and 1943. Long stretches

Ceremony attended the B-17F *Memphis Belle*, sent home in June 1943 after finishing a tour of 25 missions. As a motion picture camera wheels past its lens, General Ira C. Eaker reviews the crew, with pilot Robert K. Morgan standing ahead of the men. AAF photo

of inclement weather dogged Eighth Air Force in two ways: it could hamper or thwart altogether the efforts of forming up bombers over England for missions, and it could spread an opaque blanket across the Continent that made visual precision bombing impossible. The development of bombing radar eased the problem caused by clouds over Europe, although Eighth Air Force usually reserved radar-bombing missions for targets in Germany, and not the occupied countries, where collateral damage could have harmed innocent residents of friendly, though temporarily occupied, lands.

Into this thicket of difficulties were occasionally introduced target priorities Eighth Air Force would not have chosen as worthy of a sustained strategic campaign against Germany. Arguably tactical in nature, the campaign against German submarine pens and construction facilities was a task given to the VIII Bomber Command in 1942, when the command's assets were low. If the B-17s were associated with the attacks on the sub pens, early Eighth Air Force B-24 Liberator units were diverted from strategic bombing in order to use their long range over the ocean, seeking and destroying German submarines at sea. Again in the summer of 1944, Eighth Air Force heavy bombers would be diverted from their chosen strategic targets to participate in a campaign against elusive V-1 buzz bomb launch sites in France. That season also saw Eighth's aircraft tasked to hit targets in support of the Normandy invasion.

Though the markings indicate 34th Bomb Group, this B-17G *Flying Dutchmen* may have been a hand-me-down to the 490th Bomb Group when the photo was taken in 1945. Typically, chin turret guns were stowed pointed 90 degrees to the right when on the ground. USAFA/Brown

Left: The famous *Memphis Belle,* the only known Eighth Air Force B-17F combat veteran extant, survived a subsequent stateside tour followed by training duties. Nearly scrapped at war's end, the *Belle* was rescued and moved to a display in Memphis, Tennessee. At this location, its condition varied over the years until it was extensively refurbished. The *Memphis Belle* remained in Memphis and became the focus of a display in a new shelter on Mud Island, located in the Mississippi River, in 1987. Phil Starcer, the nephew of the *Memphis Belle*'s original nose artist, Tony Starcer, repainted the characteristic artwork on the restored bomber just before the display was unveiled. Photo by Frederick A. Johnsen

The people of Eighth Air Force addressed these hurdles with diligence and occasional inventiveness. When inroads were made by the fledgling Twelfth Air Force to secure flying units from the Eighth, the Eighth complied but lodged succinct protests up the chain of command that such depredations on its inventory would hamper Eighth Air Force's ability to do its job. At one point in 1942, General Dwight D. Eisenhower ordered Eighth Air Force to suspend all operations in the United Kingdom in order to support Twelfth Air Force and the North Africa campaign. General Spaatz protested in a manner convincing enough to prompt General Eisenhower to reverse that order on September 5, 1942.[8]

The drain of assets and manpower toward Twelfth Air Force felt by Eighth Air Force prompted some remarkably candid wartime comments in a pro-Eighth Air Force book published in 1943. *Target: Germany – The Army Air Forces' Official Story of the VIII Bomber Command's First Year over Europe* describes hard times in England when Eighth Air Force was responsible for servicing aircraft for the nascent Twelfth Air Force. Sometimes battle-damaged Eighth Air Force bombers could not be repaired quickly because maintenance men were stretched thin trying to service aircraft for both Eighth and Twelfth Air Force use.[9]

The asset and manpower drain suffered by Eighth Air Force because of Twelfth Air Force's simultaneous needs

Memphis Belle **pilot Robert K. Morgan thanks the ground crew who kept his B-17F in the fray before he departs with the storied bomber for a stateside tour in June 1943. Eighth Air Force leaders noted in wartime writings that the demands placed on their maintenance teams by the newborn Twelfth Air Force adversely impacted their ability to keep the Eighth operationally ready.** AAF/NARA

was largely over by mid-1943. At this point, units were no longer being reassigned out of the Eighth, and American production efficiencies were making more aircraft and parts available to all. Still, that summer the Eighth Air Force temporarily had to do without the badly needed strength of the 389th Bomb Group, a new Eighth Air Force Liberator unit sent first to North Africa to support the impending Ploesti low-level mission. On June 27, the 44th Bomb Group took its B-24Ds from England to North Africa to further bolster the Ploesti strike force.

The many new B-17Fs and B-24s available during 1943 were not yet matched in numbers by escort fighters of sufficient range to take the air war deep into Germany. Eighth Air Force planners and their engineering compatriots within other AAF organizations were working on that issue diligently, creating a series of large drop tanks to increase the fuel capacity of escort fighters. These tanks enabled P-38 and P-47 fighters to make some inroads over Germany, but the ultimate long-range escort fighter, the P-51 Mustang, would not achieve its full stride in fights over Berlin until early 1944.

Weather was a phenomenon never totally surmounted by new applications of technology. Some missions were scrapped due to inclement flying weather right up to the end of fighting over Europe. Forecasters assigned to

Stripped of paint and turrets, *Silver Queen* (probably serial number 42-29780) performed transport duties in the European Theater of Operations. Fortresses were favorites of general officers for transportation, and this one may have served General Curtis LeMay at 3rd Bombardment Division. According to some stories, when this aircraft's olive General drab paint was stripped, it became the first natural metal-finish B-17 in the Eighth Air Force. USAFA/Brown collection

Eighth Air Force figured only 73 days in a year had weather that would permit visual bombing of targets in Germany. That works out to only one-fifth of the year, an ineffective number of opportunities to develop a viable strategic bombardment campaign.[10] But the periods of inactivity caused by cloud cover over Europe during the early days of the Eighth Air Force's deployment prompted the AAF to exploit British H2S radar sets. Combined with increasing numbers of missions over Germany, radar mounted in select B-24s and B-17s enabled whole formations to drop bombs on the guidance of a handful of radar-equipped Pathfinder bombers. Growing out of a cadre of Pathfinders from the 482nd Bomb Group shared by other units, by October 24, 1944, the radar-equipped B-17s and B-24s were assigned to bomb groups throughout the Eighth Air Force.[11]

The growth of Eighth Air Force and its juggernaut presence in the skies over Europe would be remarkable even had there been no diversions or dilutions in the course of the war. Given the unplanned setbacks that dogged the Eighth well into 1944, the accomplishments are even more heroic.

The high squadron is in contrail-producing conditions in this 1st Bomb Division B-17 formation. Frequent cloud cover above Germany necessitated rapid development and deployment of bombing radar to enable the Eighth Air Force to keep up its campaign of precision bombing. Malcolm Gougon collection, Flight Test Historical Museum

B-17 Flying Fortress

It's bombs away for Triangle U-emblazoned B-17s of the 457th Bomb Group. Simple hinged bomb bay doors of the B-17 were prominent when opened, unlike roll-up B-24 doors. Malcolm Gougon collection via Flight Test Historical Museum

A steady parade of B-17s returns to the 490th Bomb Group's airfield in Eye, England, following a mission. Two Forts are on the runway, a third is on short final approach, and eight more hold formation for orderly timing overhead. Such air discipline was necessary for traffic control; nonetheless, Eighth Air Force suffered nonbattle losses from collisions over England. USAFA/Brown

Popular culture has already ordained the B-17 Flying Fortress as *the* American bomber icon of World War II. This veteran of both political and military struggles earned many accolades in its decade of service as a bomber. Eighth Air Force leaders including General Doolittle championed the B-17 as their first choice to carry the war to the Germans.

The development of the B-17 by Boeing in the 1930s was a timely occurrence that gave Air Corps planners of the era a vehicle on which to premise their case for long-range strategic bombardment as a war-winning tool. It was an era of stingy congressional budgets challenging heady Air Corps optimism that strategic bombers like the brand-new Boeing B-17 could decide future wars. If old-line army-navy planners were loath to embrace strategic aerial warfare as the wave of the future, the visionary bomber advocates of the 1930s were nonetheless naive in their protestations that bomber formations could be impervious to enemy challenges.

Less than a month after the first flight of the Model 299 prototype for the B-17 series, it was obvious the new four-engine Boeing had forever raised the expectations of bomber advocates when it flew nonstop from Seattle, Washington, to Wright Field, Ohio, at a record groundspeed of 233 miles per hour on August 20, 1935. The feat was all the more amazing since the contemporary operational American fighter of the day, Boeing's own monoplane P-26, had a *top* speed only 1 mile per hour faster than the big bomber's average speed on its 2,100 mile sprint from the West Coast to Ohio.[1] Add altitude and range into the mix, and the Air Corps' euphoric predictions for strategic bombardment become even more understandable.

As the developing Air Corps sought a firm footing in an American military establishment led by generals and admirals who seemed to appreciate airpower only as an adjunct to their traditional army and

***Boss Lady* of the 100th Bomb Group needed maintenance on the Number 2 engine following a mission. Though vast airfields were built in England to handle the influx of Eighth Air Force machines, much maintenance had to be conducted outdoors where the bombers parked.** USAFA/Brown

***Butch* of the 34th Bomb Group featured a dragon machine-gunning foes while riding a bomb.** USAFA/Brown

Did any image ever capture the spectacle of concentrated flak as well as this photo of Eighth Air Force B-17s turning en masse through a barrage that blackens the sky? Mission route planning endeavored to warn bomber crews of the locations of known flak battery concentrations, but those concentrations logically occurred near lucrative targets. AAF photo via Malcolm Gougon collection, Flight Test Historical Museum

Sperry A-1 upper turret on a B-17 was filled with guns and a large K-3 computing gunsight, behind which a Boeing employee peers at the camera in this Seattle flightline photo. The twin .50-caliber machine guns have been wrapped for ferrying the new bomber. Ammunition capacity totaled about 750 rounds. Boeing photo

Even direction-finding loop antenna teardrop housings were candidates for sharkmouths, as seen on *Royal Flush!* Serving with the 303rd Bomb Group, and later the 91st Bomb Group, this B-17F (42-5132) was a combat loss over the North Sea on June 22, 1943. U.S. Army Signal Corps

A single puff of German flak is visible to contest the presence of bomb-dropping B-17Gs from the 457th Bomb Group. Malcolm Gougon collection via Flight Test Historical Museum

navy, long-range strategic bombardment was an attractive role that only an evolved air force could perform. With bombardment advocates ascendant, even Air Corps fighter development suffered. This would haunt the mighty Eighth Air Force early in the war when the need for long-range escort fighters initially could not be met. And the need for those escort fighters was manifest once combat showed that bombers like the vaunted B-17s no longer possessed performance advantages over fighters of the day.[2]

The untimely loss of the company prototype Model 299 in a crash on October 30, 1935, at Wright Field was a blow to the Air Corps, but proponents of the Flying Fortress did not abandon the aircraft. An order for 13 Y1B-17s for service testing followed, with the first of these flying in December 1936. Similar in appearance to the original 299, the Y1B-17s introduced a major change in the breed by switching from 750 horsepower Pratt and Whitney Hornet engines to Wright Cyclones of, initially, 930 horsepower. Landing gear and armament revisions, as well as a change in crew complement, were also part of the legacy of these service test Fortresses.

B-17 models A through D were ordered in small quantities as dictated by pre-war budgets; the largest run was the 1940 purchase of 42 D-models. These versions all retained a strong resemblance to the prototype 299. Salient changes over this evolutionary period included the addition of turbo-superchargers starting with the lone Y1B-17A's engines for better altitude performance, a revised bombardier's nose glazing beginning with the B-models, and self-sealing fuel tanks installed on the D-models. All of these features would be present on the first Eighth Air Force combat Fortress, the B-17E.

(left) Sergeants H. G. Cleary and J. P. Danko, gunners in the 385th Bomb Group, stood beneath an enclosed B-17 right waist-gun window on April 14, 1944. Heavy ribbing supports a K-5 gun mount with coiled springs to offset the weight of the gun and keep it at neutral elevation when at rest. Ahead of the enclosed window is a closed, thin vertical wind deflector that could be extended into the slipstream when this had been an open-air waist window. USAFA/Brown collection

(below) Iron coffee-can size sheetmetal fairing of K-6 gun mount allowed this mount to shield wind blast in an enclosed Plexiglas waist window on a B-17G. Flexible feed chute reaches from a wooden ammo box. Gently curved armor plate beneath the waist window provides additional protection for the gunner. Non-computing optical N-8 gunsight rides atop the weapon's Bell E-11 recoil adapter. Boeing photo

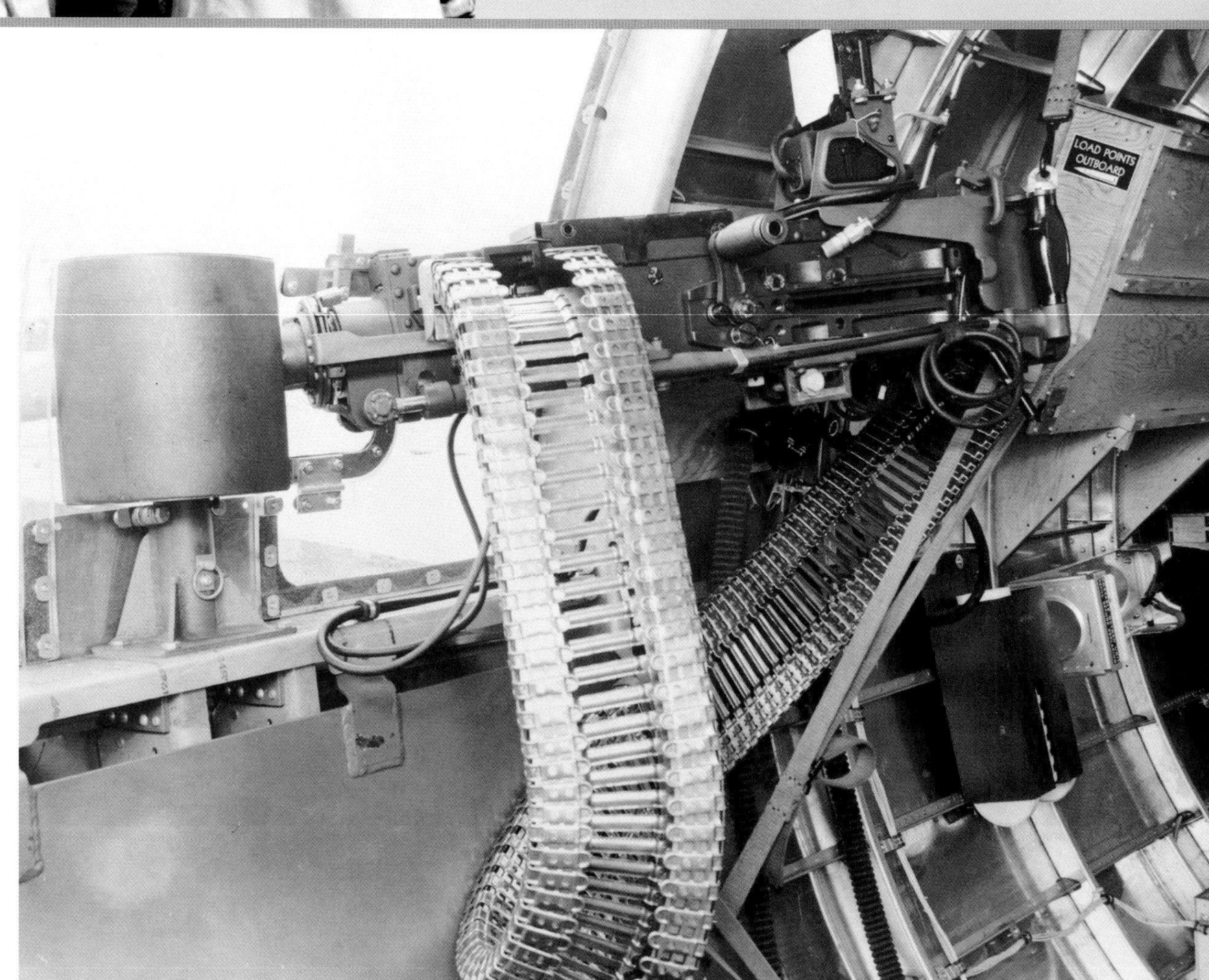

Twenty-year-old Staff Sergeant Robert L. Taylor posed in an Eighth Air Force B-17 waist section littered with empty .50-caliber brass shell casings. The wooden ammunition crate on the floor behind Taylor suggests this was a staged photo to depict combat conditions. The heavy flak apron provided some lateral protection to the gunner. AAF/NARA

A B-17E veteran of early Eighth Air Force use, *Tugboat Annie* had suffered a crumpled chin and bent props when photographed on a rainy English hardstand. This may be the former *Phyllis* of the 97th Bomb Group before transfer to the 303rd Bomb Group. Harry Fisher

The ghosted Plexiglas depression in the upper nose to accommodate a single .50-caliber machine gun is visible in this side view of *Lightning Strikes*, a B-17F photographed at the 91st Bomb Group's base at Bassingbourne, England, on October 9, 1943. USAF photo

B-17 aircrew members attend a briefing during the shuttle bombing of German targets, which involved temporary use of Soviet airfields in an edgy alliance. USAFA/Brown

B-17E

With updated insignia, the unarmed B-17E *Yankee Doodle* stayed in England after its combat days were over. This icon of the first Eighth Air Force heavy bombing mission from England earned attention in the British press for its all-American nickname. The faint pattern of Royal Air Force–style camouflage is still evident in the photo.
Erwin Steele, 91st Bomb Group

The B-17E, first flown on September 5, 1941, represented a serious acknowledgment that the Flying Fortress needed better defensive armament in the face of increasingly capable fighters. For the first time, Sperry power turrets protected the upper and lower hemispheres of the Fortress, while a tail gunner now crouched beneath a redesigned and enlarged vertical fin, where he manned a pair of .50-caliber machine guns at the extreme rear of the bomber.[3]

All previous B-17s had relied on manually moved, flexibly mounted machine guns of .30- and .50-caliber for defense. The B-17E's Sperry upper and lower turrets represented American efforts to create power turrets capable of quickly tracking fast fighters, allowing turret gunners to bring a pair of heavy .50-caliber machine guns to bear on the enemy interceptors. Though a few .30-caliber socket-mounted machine guns were employed in the noses of some B-17Es and follow-on F-models, it was the hefty M-2 .50-caliber aircraft machine gun that would be decisive in combat.

The first 112 B-17Es were fitted with a remotely sighted Sperry belly turret that, unfortunately, could promote disorientation for the gunner. The storied Sperry ball turret, in which the gunner was encapsulated and moved with his weapons in all axes, was a marked improvement that became standard from the 113th B-17E to the end of Fortress production in 1945. Photos of the first B-17Es sent into combat by the Eighth Air Force show the presence of manned ball turrets.

The B-17E had a cruise speed of 210 miles per hour and a top speed listed at 317 miles per hour. Its range with 4,000 pounds of bombs was 2,000 miles. Even as E-models first rumbled over the European Continent in the late summer of 1942, an improved Flying Fortress, the B-17F, was in the offing.

The Eighth Air Force had a number of secret weapons, not the least of which were morale-boosting mascots ranging from a donkey, to a bear, to this spaniel evidently being lectured by a 385th Bomb Group crew beside their B-17F on April 27, 1944. USAFA/Brown

One way to raise a bellied-in Flying Fortress was to insert collapsible air bladders under parts of its structure and then slowly inflate them. B-17F *Messie Bessie* (42-30152) gets a lift on December 12, 1943. AAF

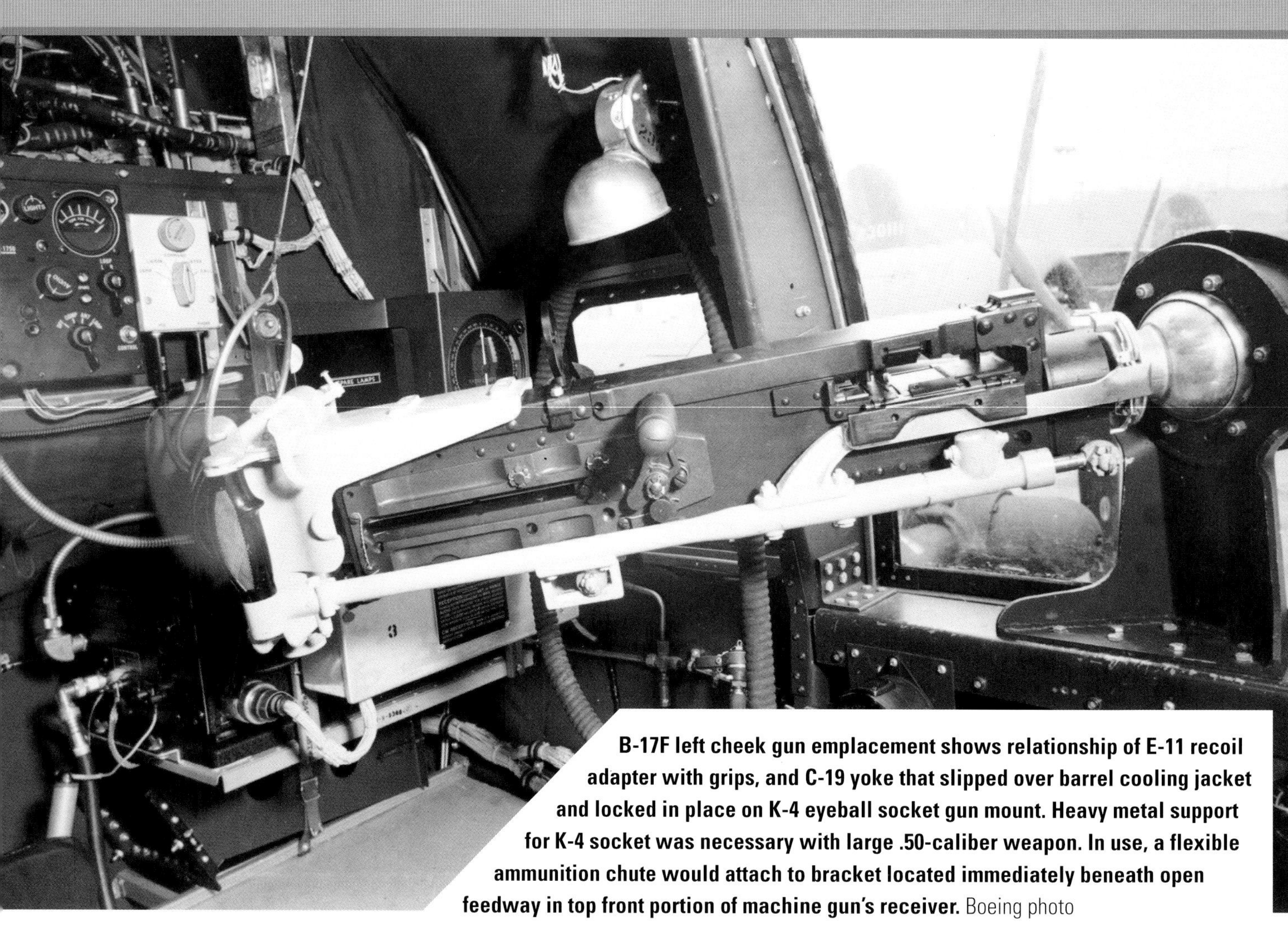

B-17F left cheek gun emplacement shows relationship of E-11 recoil adapter with grips, and C-19 yoke that slipped over barrel cooling jacket and locked in place on K-4 eyeball socket gun mount. Heavy metal support for K-4 socket was necessary with large .50-caliber weapon. In use, a flexible ammunition chute would attach to bracket located immediately beneath open feedway in top front portion of machine gun's receiver. Boeing photo

Dulled markings on this 94th Bomb Group Douglas-built B-17F (42-3259), *SNAFU*, were an effort to limit the visibility of Eighth Air Force aircraft to the Germans. The barely visible code XM in front of the national insignia denotes the 332nd Bomb Squadron. The photo predates the mid-1943 adoption of geometric tail symbols. AAF via Al Lloyd

B-17F

The F-model, at first recognizable by its elongated Plexiglas nosepiece with no metal reinforcing ribs, also used wider paddle-type propeller blades for better performance at high altitudes, and self-sealing oil tanks. During B-17F production, fuel capacity was increased by 1,100 gallons with the addition of so-called "Tokyo tanks" in previously empty outboard wing space. The Eighth Air Force hit its stride in the procurement of B-17Fs in 1943. The first model of the Fortress to be produced at additional manufacturers other than Boeing in Seattle, the B-17F's production totaled 3,405, which dwarfed the production run of only 512 B-17Es. The F-model could cruise at 200 miles per hour and had a top speed of 299 miles per hour. Tokyo tanks added nominally 200 miles to the range of F-models so equipped to the range of B-17Es. The needs of combat in Europe dictated additional equipment and increasing amounts of armor for crew protection. The bane of aircraft designers—upward-creeping aircraft weight—made its presence felt on B-17s, and speed suffered.

***Tinker Toy*, a B-17F of the 381st Bomb Group, suffered major nose damage on October 8, 1943, in a mission to Bremen, Germany, then beyond the range of friendly escort fighters. FW-190 fighters made point-blank attacks, and some of their 20-mm cannon rounds found their way into the cockpit of *Tinker Toy*, decapitating the hapless pilot.** USAF

Pride of the Kiarians **became a source of parts for other Eighth Air Force B-17s, and a source of amusement for a staff sergeant who provided a unique size comparison by leaning out of the left cheek-gun window opening of this cannibalized B-17F. Air depots in England repaired the aircraft of the Eighth Air Force, often by recycling good parts from salvaged airplanes.** Air Force photo

This experimental 20-millimeter cannon installation in the nose of a 385th Bomb Group B-17F was photographed in August 1943. The drum atop the gun is an ammunition magazine. Heavy bracing and cables were installed to tame the powerful recoil of the cannon, but the installation did not gain favor. AAF via Jeffrey L. Kolln collection

The broad wing of the Flying Fortress contributed to the B-17's structural integrity. In the photo, circa summer of 1943, paint around the bulged astrodome on top of the nose of this B-17F appears newer than the surrounding finish, possibly indicating a field installation in place of an earlier-style flat window in this location. USAFA/Brown collection

PEGGY D, 97th Bomb Group

B-17F *Holy Mackeral* performs an engine run at Eccles Row in Norfolk on July 15, 1943. Differing from most camouflaged B-17s, the gray lower surfaces of the engine cowlings extend all the way to the cowl ring on this Fortress.

Not all Eighth Air Force losses were due to combat; taxiing accidents like the one that severed B-17F *King Bee* on December 27, 1943, contributed to attrition as surely as enemy action. USAFA/Brown collection

Safe at home with a guard posted, the 25-mission B-17F *Memphis Belle* rested at Washington's National Airport on June 16, 1943, upon a triumphant return from combat over Europe. NARA

MEMPHIS BELLE, 91st Bomb Group

Roger Dodg'-her, a B-17F with late-style cheek guns in K-5 mounts, may have served with the 94th Bomb Group. The light passing through holes in the cheek-gun cooling jacket suggests that the barrel assembly has been removed for cleaning. USAFA/Brown

This close-up of the right waist window on *Memphis Belle* shows a typical B-17F waist opening, with the edge of the sliding hatch visible toward the front of the window. When the *Belle* left England in June 1943 for a U.S. tour, it was liberally autographed by AAF well-wishers. Claims for two Luftwaffe fighters downed are noted by the two swastikas painted nearby. AAF/NARA

YB-40

The tested-in-combat YB-40 Fortress escort gunships reverted to miscellaneous duty, including training, after they were withdrawn from Eighth Air Force combat service. This example, serial number 42-5741, was forced to abort the first escort mission to St. Nazaire, France, on May 29, 1943, when the Number 2 engine's turbo-supercharger developed problems.

In 1942, the Eighth's bomber offensive faced several difficult options, ranging from unacceptably high attrition to pulling missions away from the well-defended German homeland.

A Flying Fortress called the XB-40, flew into Eglin Field, Florida, on November 19, set to prove it had the range to run interference with the Luftwaffe all the way to the target. In a wartime whirlwind trial, the XB-40's armaments were tested in six days and found to be generally satisfactory.[4]

The purpose of the B-40 was to act as a heavy escort fighter, strategically nested in a formation of bombers, and using its extra guns and an overload of ammunition to ward off enemy fighter attacks. It soon showed itself to be stopgap at best, until nimble escort fighters could be developed. As evaluated in Eighth Air Force service, the B-40 carried no offensive bombs—only defensive ammunition. Its sole contribution to the war effort was to throw up a curtain of gunfire to keep the Luftwaffe at bay. The typical combat ammunition load for a YB-40 variant was 11,000 rounds, up to as many as 17,000 rounds.

Following the XB-40, Douglas Aircraft in Oklahoma modified 19 YB-40 service-test versions and 4 TB-40 trainers. In October 1942, when Major General Muir S. Fairchild, the AAF's director of military requirements, requested that the Proving Ground look into staggering the waist windows openings on the B-40 to give each gunner more room to move.[5]

Twelve YB-40s flew combat in the Eighth Air Force's 92nd Bomb Group between May and August 1943. The operational crews of the 92nd Bomb Group quickly learned it took more gasoline for the laden YB-40s to climb and hold formation with regular B-17Fs.

For all their guns and ammunition, the YB-40s posted a tally sheet of only five German aircraft claimed destroyed, two probable kills, and seven damaged during their trial by fire in the summer of 1943.[6]

If the YB-40s were not the answer to the Eighth Air Force's escort problems, they did show some defensive armament trends that would appear on production B-17 bombers later. The Bendix chin turret stood out as a winner, it was an armament that helped dissuade some German fighter pilots from pressing the head-on attacks they had relied on previously. The doubled-up armament in the waist and the second dorsal turret on the YB-40s were deemed unnecessary. Staggered waist windows, used on YB-40s, would be introduced during B-17G production, as would the chin turret.

B-17G

HIHIN' FOR HOME, 91th Bomb Group

Its prominent chin turret, reminiscent of the earlier YB-40 escort variants, characterized the final production model of the Flying Fortress, the B-17G. Gross weight of the G-model was highest of the series at 65,500 pounds, more than five tons heavier than that of the B-17F. Cruising speed was down to 182 miles per hour, and top speed was posted as 287 miles per hour. The three assembly lines turned out 8,680 B-17Gs. The first flew on May 21, 1943; production ended at Boeing's Seattle plant as well as at Douglas and Vega in April 1945.

The continued utility of the B-17G in combat over Germany up to war's end can be attributed to more than simply an inspired design. Worthy as the B-17G was, its survivability in 1945 was due in part to the AAF's concerted efforts to render the Luftwaffe helpless. The 1944 introduction of P-51 Mustangs able to reach deep into Germany gave the Eighth Air Force bombers the kind of aggressive fighter support they needed to successfully prosecute the war.

Majestic natural metal-finish B-17Gs of the 381st Bomb Group exhibit both types of tail gun positions used on the last Fortress production model. The aircraft nearest to camera has the improved Cheyenne modification with greater field of fire than on the factory-style tail stinger of the distant Fortress. AAF via Al Lloyd

The 91st Bomb Group's Triangle-A tail markings identify these natural metal-finish B-17Gs in formation over Europe. USAF photo

A fire truck rushes toward a belly-landed B-17G (42-97376) of the 95th Bomb Group on May 30, 1944, at Honington. Only one engine—Number 3 on the near wing—has an unbent propeller blade, indicating it was shut down when the mishap occurred. With its low-mounted wing built with a stout internal truss structure, Boeing's B-17 was a relatively easy aircraft to belly land with minimal damage. AAF via Bob Sturges collection

A lieutenant in a button-up leather jacket posed for a snapshot with the 388th Bomb Group's B-17G *Punchin' Judy*. Jeffrey Kolln collection

Returning from a mission to Brest, France, on August 26, 1944, a B-17G from the 388th Bomb Group is framed in the circular propeller arc of a fellow Fortress in a color slide taken by airman Mark Brown. What was routine in 1944 now has the impact of time travel; this color image brings World War II to life again. Brown collection

Luck ran out for *Little Miss Mischief*, a 91st Bomb Group B-17G resurrected out of parts from more than one bomber. By April 1945, the Fortress looked like this; it was forlornly dragged to the side and ultimately scrapped. USAF

Before acquiring the unit markings of the 96th Bomb Group, Boeing's milestone B-17G *5 Grand* was photographed in flight on Kodachrome film. From a distance, the aluminum bomber seems to have a tinted sheen. Up close, this is the effect of thousands of signatures of Boeing workers painted in various colors on the B-17 before it left the factory for combat. Since the Pearl Harbor attack, *5 Grand* was the 5,000th B-17 built by Boeing. AAF photo

B-17G, 401st BOMB GROUP

Battle damage blocked movement of the ball-turret guns on this 447th Bomb Group Fortress (probably B-17G-BO number 42-31227), causing them to scribe the pavement as the ripped bomber landed. A direct hit on the radio room during the March 6, 1944, mission to Berlin caused the carnage. USAFA/Brown collection

Peeled aluminum skin beside the radio room and other evidence of metal mangling were visible when this 447th Bomb Group B-17G, 42-31227, returned from Berlin. USAFA/Brown collection

Opposite page: A rushing jet of flame marks an imperiled radar-equipped 447th Bomb Group B-17G, high over snow-covered terrain. Tales of the Flying Fortresses' durability could not ward off all dangers in the skies over Europe. AAF/Brown collection

Given the opportunity, B-17 pilots would prefer to belly land on one of England's expansive grass fields. But that wasn't to be when *Super Rabbit*, a B-17G (possibly from the 351st Bomb Group), slid on the pavement on July 28, 1944. The aluminum chin turret tub and the rest of the chin turret structure were mashed into the nose. USAFA/Brown

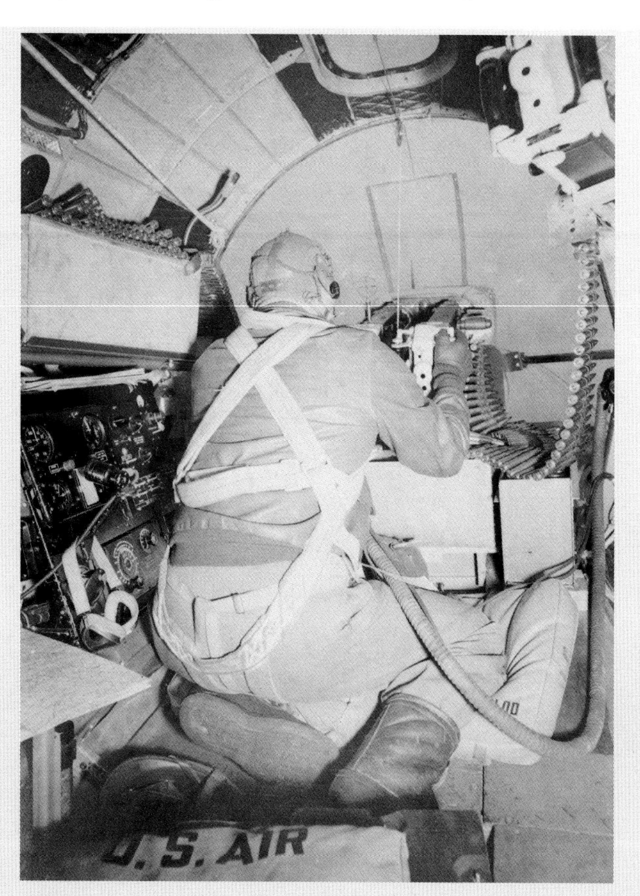

An Eighth Air Force bombardier took a turn at the flexible .50-caliber nose guns in his B-17F, circa December 1943. In this aircraft, the answer to Luftwaffe head-on attacks came from a pair of guns mounted close to the aircraft's centerline, with Bell E-11 recoil adapters absorbing some of the shock. AAF/NARA

A head-on B-17F view shows the indented forward flexible gun mount in the upper nose using a K-4 ball socket in a reinforced structure.

The global nature of World War II meant the weapons of war could not all be cookie-cutter copies of each other; aircraft like the B-17 evolved in service as needs that were specific to a particular locale or mission manifested themselves. It was not always possible to introduce new upgrades on the assembly line without faltering in the pace of production. As a result, many basic B-17s left the factory not quite ready for combat. They received upgraded armaments and equipment at designated stateside modification centers, or even after arriving in the United Kingdom. The celebrated American trait of inventiveness—call it Yankee ingenuity or simply an innate can-do outlook—produced some field modifications in the Eighth Air Force that adapted B-17s to fight in that theater.

Evident in Eighth Air Force B-17 evolution was a series of frontal gun emplacement modifications applied to B-17Fs before the advent of chin-turreted G-models. As early as November 1942, German fighter pilots began shifting away from the classic rear attacks in favor of head-on plunges through Fortress and Liberator formations. The incredible combined closing speeds of these attacks gave little room for error. If a headlong rush into a group of B-17s held the possibility of collision, it also reduced the ability of early Fortress models to bring effective guns to bear on the German fighters in the few seconds of confrontation.

Soon after the Luftwaffe made its troubling turn toward head-on attack tactics, B-17Fs began arriving in

Upgrades usually seen on B-17Gs, including ribbed, enclosed waist windows with K-5 gun mounts and possibly a K-5 enclosed radio-room gun, are evident on this B-17F (42-30195) photographed at Honington on July 19, 1944. When the enclosed waist-window frame was installed, it intruded into the bar of the national insignia. The square "H" emblem on the tail indicates the 388th Bomb Group. AAF via Bob Sturges collection

England. F-models, with their longer Plexiglas noses, conducted the first American attack against Germany proper on January 27, 1943, when they bombed Wilhelmshaven. Early F-models went to war with at least one lightweight .30-caliber machine gun suspended from a socket supported only by the Plexiglas of the nose. At Boeing, by the time Block 55 of B-17F production was being built, two flexible cheek guns were added on each side of the nose just behind the Plexiglas nose cap. The other two builders of B-17s also added .50-caliber cheek guns during F-model production. The heavy .50-caliber machine guns could not be suspended from the unreinforced Plexiglas nose; hence the move to cheek windows, where heavy mounts in the fuselage structure could support the guns.

But early cheek-window guns were still not optimal for frontal attacks, since their field of fire was restricted by the nature of their K-4 ball mounts in the gently tapering nose of the B-17F. Two forms of relief ensued. Late B-17Fs carried their cheek guns in windows with a stout metal frame that protruded out from the fuselage contour far enough to allow a K-5 gun mount to hold the gun in a position more nearly straight ahead than previously possible. (This installation may have been pioneered on the service-test YB-40s sent to England in the summer of 1943. Another F-model cheek window used slightly bulged Plexiglas to accommodate a gun mount with additional forward sweep, compared to the older flush style.) The ultimate forward-firing .50-caliber installation on Eighth Air Force B-17Fs employed a steel tubing truss inside the nose capable of supporting a single .50-caliber machine gun that gave a cone-of-fire protection directly in front of the Fortress. This involved a deep inset in the upper portion of the nose that is clearly visible in photos of many Eighth Air Force F-models. Eighth Air Force chronicler Roger A. Freeman attributes the standardizing of a single nose-mounted .50-caliber flexible gun in B-17Fs for full-frontal protection to the efforts of two staff sergeants from the 306th Bomb Group, Ben Marcilonis and James Green. They worked on B-17 frontal armament in their spare time in December 1942. One was an armorer, the other a welder, and their combined expertise resulted in a viable mount.

Localized modifications took place on some Fortresses in Eighth Air Force bomb groups. Hinged doors covering the strike camera in 390th Bomb Groups B-17s

Darker olive-drab paint around this cheek-gun window framing suggests this was a field installation made after original olive-drab paint on the rest of this B-17 had begun to fade. *Our Gal Sal* flew with the 100th Bomb Group, logging more than 100 missions before returning to peacetime storage, and ultimately scrapping, in the United States. USAFA/Brown

Flexible articulated stainless steel ammunition chutes draped in the nose of a new B-17G on the Boeing flight-line feed the two cheek guns from ammo storage boxes mounted in the nose. The aluminum chin turret tub conceals two large curved ammunition cans to serve the .50-caliber machine guns of that turret. Although the aircraft has been built in natural metal finish, the supply of Bendix chin turrets is still in gray paint as of this April 1944 image. Boeing photo

Boots encircled by mission bombs adorned the aptly nicknamed *Boots IV*, a B-17G (42-37850) of the 96th Bomb Group. Brown via Al Lloyd

This post-combat photo remains enigmatic. It shows substantial damage to a reinforced concrete sub pen, part of a series identified by the photographer as being at Farge below Vegesack, Germany. Given the lack of serious damage standard U.S. bombs inflicted on the reinforced German submarine facilities, this crater looks to be the work of a special piece of ordnance. An AAF report states that rocket-boosted Disney bombs were used on concrete maritime targets in this geographic location near war's end, leading to speculation that this is where one of those special bombs came hurtling back to earth. However, the available caption is not conclusive. USAFA/Brown collection

With art deco license taken in the design of the letter H on its tail, this 388th Bomb Group B-17G (42-102435) releases its bombs. Kolln collection

Before standardizing the ball turret opening as the site for radar, H2S sets were sometimes mounted in large fairings beneath the noses of B-17Fs. Deployment of reliable bombing radar was necessary to permit the Eighth Air Force to keep pressure on targets in Germany whenever cloud cover ruined the chance for visual bombing. AFHRA

An early hand-built iteration of H2X bombing radar is shown nested behind the chin turret of an Eighth Air Force B-17. The ultimate location for radar was in the spot normally occupied by the lower ball turret. AFHRA

were removed to avoid the possibility of the doors remaining closed during a bomb run. Some Eighth Air Force B-17s used in night operations had flash hiders attached to the muzzles of their machine guns.

Near the end of fighting over Europe, Eighth Air Force operationally tested a rocket-assisted concrete-piercing bomb known as Disney. Conventional American 2,000-pound bombs had shown little effect against the reinforced concrete of German maritime facilities. Disney was a British invention of Royal Navy Captain Edward Terrell. Weighing 4,500 pounds, the Disney bomb was released as any other bomb, but at 5,000 feet above ground, rocket motors accelerated the Disney device to a speed of 2,400 feet per second at impact. This gave the bomb enough momentum to penetrate 20 feet into concrete before exploding. The weight and size of each Disney bomb dictated that bomb range was limited and it had to be shackled externally beneath the wings of B-17s.[7]

After the 92nd Bomb Group tried the large, slender devices on a captured heavy concrete structure in France, Eighth Air Force dropped several Disneys operationally in March 1945. According to a declassified AAF paper: "Four combat missions had been carried out up to 3 April employing the 4500 lb. Disney (rocket-assisted concrete-piercing) bomb. The first three were on 'E' boat pens at Ijmuiden, Holland. In each mission a force of nine Eighth Air Force B-17s was employed, and the bombing was done by flights of three planes. Excellent accuracy was obtained. The fourth mission was against the U-boat pens at Farge, Germany, where a group of 36 B-17s dropped 72 Disneys."[8]

Results were not immediately available from the 36-ship mission, but earlier nine-plane attacks produced evidence of damage that was encouraging. It was also reported that penetration in open soil was about 200 feet. Ultimately, Allied advances on the shrinking German territory removed the need for more Disney attacks.

Eighth Air Force heavy bombers like these silhouetted B-17Gs sometimes performed airdrop sorties over enemy territory on the Continent to resupply partisans. In a Kodachrome image almost lyrical in its juxtaposition of bombers with pastoral sun-dappled countryside, supply parachutes can be seen blossoming beneath the Fortresses on September 9, 1944. Supply drops often were made at slow speeds with landing gear down. USAFA/Brown

Paint and Markings

Some B-17Es served in England with two-tone camouflaged upper surfaces over light blue-gray undersurfaces. Markings specialist Dana Bell describes Eighth Air Force B-17E colors as comparable to Royal Air Force Dark Earth and Dark Green over Deep Sky Blue, a U.S. shade rendered as a light pastel blue. Other Eighth Air Force E-models wore more typical AAF colors of olive-drab uppers over neutral gray undersides.[9] Some early Eighth Air Force B-17s initially carried large 'U.S. ARMY' lettering on the underside of the wings, presumably in insignia blue. Photos of 97th Bomb Group B-17Es with RAF-style camouflaging show a wavy demarcation line between undersurfaces and uppers instead of the usual straight, feathered demarcation of most camouflaged B-17s.

B-17Fs were initially factory painted olive drab over neutral gray. Many Eighth Air Force F-models subsequently received irregular blotching of medium green, especially around the edges of straight wing and tail surfaces, to break up geometric patterns as a way of enhancing camouflage. As olive drab faded in the sun, it often turned more tan in color. Repairs and modifications to Eighth Air Force B-17Fs and olive drab G-models can sometimes be seen as darker areas of fresh olive-drab paint.

B-17Gs initially joined Eighth Air Force in olive and gray; by January 1944, they were leaving the assembly lines in natural metal finish. At that stage in the war, the need for camouflage was diminishing as Allied forces were in ascendancy toward victory. Natural-metal

***Lady Geraldine*, a B-17G of the 100th Bomb Group, carried the unit's diagonal black slash on the lower left and upper right wing surfaces. This view clearly shows the exposed lower curve of the B-17's main wheels when retracted, a feature that afforded pilots some control in wheels-up landings.** USAFA/Brown collection

Bobby Sox **adorned a silver B-17G of the 490th Bomb Group at Eye, England. The variety and occasional high quality of bomber nose art remains an intriguing subset of any research into the Eighth Air Force.** USAFA/Brown

Humpty Dumpty **was never more glamorously portrayed than in this 100th Bomb Group rendering on a silver B-17G. The one-piece Plexiglas nose cap is one of three basic styles applied to B-17Gs.** USAFA/Brown

B-17F *Big Dick* carries additional artwork on the forward crew entry and escape hatch. The irregular background around the dice on the nose may have been painted red, according to contemporary notes about this Fortress. USAFA/Brown collection

Sunny II **was chewed up in a belly landing on December 30, 1943, as part of the 100th Bomb Group (denoted by the Square D on the tail). This was a B-17F (42-30796).** USAFA/Brown collection

A letter home illustrated the B-17F wholesomely nicknamed *Dear Mom*, possibly from the 94th Bomb Group. USAFA/Brown collection

The white triangle on the tail of B-17F *Little America* indicates the 1st Bomb Division; the letter P inside is for the 384th Bomb Group. When white bars were added to the insignia in mid-1943, the bars partially covered previous identification letters. AAF/NARA

Elaborate art accompanied *Dragon Lady* into combat. Although movie portrayals often have B-17 crew members hoisting themselves in and out of the forward hatch unaided, this candid ramp photo shows a ladder placed at the entry to make that task easier. USAFA/Brown collection

Fortresses were somewhat faster and more fuel-efficient than their painted counterparts, although the natural metal "5 Grand", carrying thousands of paint signatures, surprised its ferry crew with high gasoline consumption.

The overall color of Eighth Air Force B-17s was surmounted by an evolution of national insignia and highly customized unit markings between 1942 and 1945. By the time the Eighth went to war, most U.S. aircraft had simple white stars in dark insignia blue discs on both fuselage sides as well as the upper left and lower right wing surfaces. Beginning in the fall of 1942, the bright white stars on some Eighth Air Force aircraft, ultimately to include some B-17s, were overpainted with gray to tone them down as a further enhancement to camouflage.

The next significant change to national insignia was the introduction of white rectangular bars on either side of the blue star disc, with a short-lived red outline to the whole insignia that was in effect from July to September 1943, when the red was replaced by blue. This style of insignia remained standard through the end of the war.

As more and more B-17s arrived in England to bolster the Eighth Air Force, it became increasingly necessary to identify particular aircraft and the bomb groups to which they belonged to enable orderly formations and mission execution. By December 1942, Eighth Air Force B-17s had joined other AAF aircraft in the United Kingdom in adopting the British style of recognition letters, consisting of unique two-letter designators for each squadron and a third letter that was unique to one aircraft within each squadron. The famous B-17F *Memphis Belle* is a classic example of this identifier scheme, using large yellow letters 'A*DF' on its fuselage. The 'A' was the individual aircraft identifier; the letters 'DF' signified the 324th Bomb Squadron of the 91st Bomb Group.

B-17 unit markings evolved again in May and June 1943 when the Eighth's growing number of heavy bomber groups was organized into 1st and 4th Bomb Wings (B-17s) and 2nd Bomb Wing (B-24s). The 1st Bomb Wing soon adopted a triangle, painted on the vertical fin and upper right wing, as a geometric identifier; the 4th Bomb Wing used a square, and the B-24s of the 2nd BW used a circular disc. On the olive-drab bombers, the geometric symbols were painted white or gray with a black or insignia blue letter superimposed and identifying specific groups within the wing. The wing designator changed to division on September 13, 1943. The 4th Bomb Wing was changed to become the 3rd Bomb Division at that time; it included both B-17s and B-24s in its square geometry for a period of time.

In 1944, Eighth Air Force B-17s began adopting vivid color patterns for quick bomb group identification. Squadron and individual aircraft letters still pertained, but the huge tail surfaces of the Fortresses allowed individual bomb groups to paint patterns that would be recognizable from a distance as an aid in forming up.

Some photos depict temporary letters and geometric symbols painted to B-17s circa 1943. These most likely are temporary markings of the day, used occasionally in an effort to thwart German fliers in captured B-17s from penetrating American formations for purposes of radioing information about heading and altitude back to German gunners.

Other paint subtleties show up in Eighth Air Force B-17 photos. Late F-models and camouflaged B-17Gs generally show overall upper surfaces of olive drab, without the breakup splotches of medium green applied earlier in the war. And, almost universally, camouflaged B-17 engine cowlings carried the olive drab completely around the lip of the cowling in front instead of allowing the undersurface gray to wrap around the lower lip of the cowling.

The rapid withdrawal of B-17s from combat in Europe at the end of the war signaled the inevitable: the grand old Flying Fortress was out of date. It was outclassed by bigger B-29s and threatened severely by a dawning jet age in which increasingly competent fighter aircraft would savage any propeller-driven bombers unfortunate enough to cross their paths. Yet the B-17 was not to be forgotten; it would forever remain the symbol of the mighty Eighth Air Force in World War II.

Opposite page: Two parallel yellow bars on the right upper wing surface and the Square L marking on the tail identify this B-17G (43-38989) as a part of the 452nd Bomb Group. Late war markings defied earlier quests for camouflage and used bright colors to help identify bomb groups from a distance as a formation aid. USAFA/Brown collection

An early Block-10 Vega-built B-17G in England shows with clarity where its cheek gun windows were added in the field. Faded olive drab paint altered the appearance of B-17s, lightening their color as they aged. Cheek gun is carried in a cylindrical K-5 gun mount. AAF photo

Hell's Angels, **a signature-bedecked B-17F (41-24577) of the 303rd Bomb Group, departs England for the United States after finishing combat in 1944. Actually the first Eighth Air Force B-17 to complete 25 missions, *Hell's Angels* lost the honor of touring the U.S. with its 25-mission accomplishment to the B-17F *Memphis Belle. Hell's Angels* subsequently reached the 50-mission mark.** AAF/NARA

Even children's book characters were immortalized on Eighth Air Force bombers. *Winnie the Pooh* was a B-17F. Barely visible in the Plexiglas nose is a plywood ammunition container for one of the guns.
USAFA/Brown collection

B-24 Liberator

The horrors of Eighth Air Force combat can be seen in blinding flames torching back from *Little Warrior* of the 493rd Bomb Group, struck by flak while bombing Quakenbruk on June 29, 1944. Open bomb bay doors reveal flames inside. USAF

The shadow beneath the co-pilot's side window reveals the thick armor glass that was installed on some Eighth Air Force B-24s to protect the vital cockpit area. Bolt-on armor plating also is visible just below the side windows. USAFA/Brown

The *Gemini* twins toted a bomb on the side of their B-24 from the 486th Bomb Group in the summer of 1944. USAFA/Brown

The Eighth Air Force capitalized on both American heavy bombers available continuously from 1942 to 1945. The Consolidated B-24 Liberator's design was four years younger than that of the B-17—simultaneously boon and bane for the newer Liberator. The B-24 used state-of-the-art devices more modern than some components of the older tailwheeled Flying Fortress. The Liberator's tricycle landing gear, Fowler area-increasing flaps, and Davis high-lift airfoil characterized a leap ahead in bomber technology. In fact, some of these features would appear on Boeing's next "Very Heavy Bomber," the mighty B-29 Superfortress.

But with all its design advancements, the B-24 had a much shorter time to evolve before the urgency of war rushed Liberators into combat. At the end of November 1941—only a week before Pearl Harbor was attacked—the Air Force counted 145 B-17s in its inventory, and only 11 B-24s.[1]

Of all the friendly rivalries between American combat forces of World War II, none proved so durable as the feud between B-17 and B-24 crews. While the older B-17s had enjoyed much publicity in the 1930s, the B-24s benefited from much less publicity, prompting some Liberator devotees to speak derisively of the B-17 as the "Hollywood bomber." Fortress aficionados decried the boxier appearance of the Liberator, but beauty is in the eye of the beholder.

Initially, B-24s held a distinct speed and range advantage over the B-17s. But in Eighth Air Force use, the localized requirement for additional heavy protective armor eroded this performance edge. If B-17s gained a reputation for wing-and-a-prayer ruggedness, there is some anecdotal evidence to suggest that accounts of B-24s' vulnerability have snowballed in the decades since European combat ended, and myth and exaggeration may have shaded reality.

A B-24 MPC tail turret trainer at Tonopah, Nevada, showed details of the mount in an actual cutaway B-24 fuselage. Central Nevada Historical Society

There are, however, some statistical comments in the reams of documentation turned out by different AAF

***Big Dealer* added bright colors to the dark olive hide of a Ford B-24 in England circa 1944.** Brown collection

The zodiac-themed B-24s in Eighth Air Force's 486th Bomb Group included *Pisces* toting a shackled bomb. USAFA/Brown

constituents that are less than flattering to the B-24. According to an unsigned report dated April 3, 1943, from the AAF's Statistical Control Division, Office of Management Control, comparing B-24s and B-17s:

...based on a great volume of statistical data . . . covering many aspects . . . the B-17 is very much the more valuable airplane. . . . sortie loss rates of the two models have been roughly equal. However, this is not a fair comparison because the B-24s are, on the average, sent on easier missions. This fact was confirmed in the course of a recent trip to the United Kingdom. The greater vulnerability of the B-24s is well recognized. In fairness to the respective crews and to maintain crew morale and keep down losses, the types of missions on which the two models are sent [are] deliberately balanced in such a way as to keep losses approximately equal [*sic*].

Try telling that to a veteran of European combat in a B-24.

General Jimmy Doolittle, Eighth Air Force commander in 1944 and 1945, did his best to shape the fighting force he could bring to bear against the Germans. By necessity, his roster of aircraft included more than one type of bomber and fighter. This was because the industrial might of the United States strained to deliver enough aircraft to meet, first, the needs of the European war and, second, those of Pacific combat. Thus, General Doolittle and his predecessors would have to deal with all the logistical and operational complexities of operating diverse warplanes with varying needs and abilities. Two of Doolittle's efforts at streamlining Eighth Air Force involved divesting his fighter force of P-38s, and to some extent, P-47s, in favor of P-51s and trading some Third Air Division B-24s for more B-17s. Interestingly, all three of the warplanes General Doolittle wanted to remove from his Eighth Air Force are generally recognized as war-winners in the Pacific.

General Doolittle weighed in on the European Theater B-24 issue in a lengthy letter to Lieutenant General Barney M. Giles, Army Air Forces Chief of Air Staff, on January 25, 1945:

The original B-24 would carry a greater bomb load (8000 lb against 6000 lb) than the B-17. It would carry this load farther and was faster. Upon being put into operations in the European Theater, it was found that the armament and armor of the B-24 were inadequate and in order to operate without prohibitive losses it was necessary to make emergency modifications immediately. These modifications consisted, among other things, of a formidable nose turret, which together with the other additions substantially increased the weight, reduced the aerodynamic characteristics and although increasing

An Eighth Air Force B-24 nicknamed *The Royal Flush!* carried a painting of a toilet to war. USAFA/Brown

The 44th Bomb Group's *Rugged Buggy* had toned-down star insignia when photographed in flight. This Eighth Air Force Liberator was lost on a mission to Kiel on May 14, 1943. AAF

the firepower, eventually unacceptably reduced the overall utility of the aircraft.[2]

General Doolittle went on to describe Eighth Air Force Liberators thus encumbered as having lost their initial range, altitude, and load advantages to the B-17. Particularly vexing was the addition of the nose turret that General Doolittle said hindered pilot visibility by protruding above nose contours. This problem, he said, was exacerbated by the lower speeds heavy B-24s were now forced to use over Europe, further necessitating nose-high flight to maintain lift at those speeds. Yet another difficulty experienced aboard nose-turreted B-24s, Doolittle noted, was cramped quarters and poor visibility for the bombardier and navigator in the revised nose. Interestingly, nowhere in his lengthy four-page single-space letter to General Giles did General Doolittle suggest Eighth Air Force B-24s were given less perilous missions than were the B-17s.[3]

The five Liberator groups in the Third Air Division were considered for conversion to B-17s as the opportunity arose in mid-1944.[4] Even though General Doolittle preferred Fortresses in Eighth Air Force, realities, including the emphasis on B-29 production at Boeing, home of the B-17, made it prudent for him to argue for the best possible Liberator modifications he could get in 1945. Into the last months of the European war, officials of the Eighth and Fifteenth Air Forces looked at ways to standardize their requirements for B-24 modifications to streamline the delivery of new Liberators to both organizations.[5] It is interesting to note that, while the last B-17G from Boeing was delivered on April 13, 1945, and the last Fortress of all, a Vega delivery, was recorded July 29, 1945, Convair and Ford continued building B-24 Liberators officially into May or June of that year, but actual deliveries were even later in 1945. Had the war continued, Ford would have built a production run of single-tail B-24Ns that Eighth Air Force was already contemplating early that year.[6]

Even Eighth Air Force officials had to admit there were some attributes of the B-24 Liberator that, statistically, were superior to the B-17. The Operational Analysis Section of Eighth Air Force interrogated 660 B-17 and B-24 crew members who had escaped when 228 B-17s and 54 B-24s went missing in action over Europe from the first missions of August 1942 to June 1, 1944. The crewmen were eyewitnesses to the demise of their own bombers and were able to provide clues to the causes of the aircraft losses. The statistics showed, for the bombers in the survey, B-17s suffered a 47 percent failure rate for propeller feathering, compared with a failure rate of 26 percent for B-24s. (All statistics excluded propellers that

Camouflaged Ford B-24s were characterized by a uniform wavy scalloped demarcation between gray and olive drab on their fuselages. The entire Ford nose turret and bombardier installation differed appreciably in contours from the design built in San Diego. As a result, Liberators assembled by Douglas and Convair Fort Worth from Ford-supplied knockdown kits have the Ford-style nose shape. USAFA/Brown

Several bombers were known as *Superstitious Aloysius,* including this Ford B-24, which employed Eighth Air Force armor plate beside the pilot but not in the form of bullet-resistant glass in the canopy. USAFA/Brown collection

***Virgo* continued the zodiac theme applied to a number of Eighth Air Force 486th Bomb Group B-24s, in this case overpainting half of the fire extinguisher door. Tool marks are evident from shaping the armor plate mounted beside the pilot's side of the cockpit.** USAFA/Brown

crews voluntarily allowed to windmill instead of feathering). Feathering was a crucial option for pilots when engines were knocked out of service. By feathering a propeller, its blades were pivoted at the hub to present a knife-edge to the slipstream, thereby stopping the prop from windmilling or spinning in the rushing air.[7]

The report explained:

One uncontrolled windmilling propeller on a four-engined aircraft is a potential cause of loss as it usually causes straggling. The majority of the losses occurred amongst stragglers. Straggler losses can be expected to be reduced since France came under Allied control. About 30% of windmilling propellers caused such excessive vibration that the aircraft were abandoned in flight.[8]

Both the B-17 and B-24 used the same basic propeller, which long outlived the war years, leaving no doubt about its general worthiness. Perhaps this admittedly anecdotal survey best serves as comforting evidence that, even in the cauldron of combat over Europe, B-24s were better at some things than B-17s, and Eighth Air Force was unbiased in its assessment of that fact. This many years after the end of World War II in Europe, significance clings to the deeds of airmen in both kinds of heavy bomber, regardless of any aircraft performance deficiencies, perceived or real.

B-24s ultimately were built on five assembly lines, with some peculiarities unique to each line. The Consolidated Vultee (Convair) home factory was in San Diego, California. A second Consolidated line was located in Fort Worth, Texas. Nearby, in Dallas, Texas, North American Aviation established B-24 construction under contract. A heavyweight in Liberator production was automaker Ford, with a big, modern plant in Willow Run, Michigan. In addition to its own assembly, Ford made kits to be assembled by Douglas at Tulsa, Oklahoma. Until its own production came on line, Convair Fort Worth also assembled Ford kits.

The 446th Bomb Group put up a force of olive and gray B-24s that cruised with ball turrets retracted inside their fuselages to reduce drag unless hostile aircraft were expected. USAF

As if pushed toward the target by their own brilliant contrails, Eighth Air Force B-24s forged ahead in November 1944. It is quite remarkable that large fleets of Liberators confronted Germany, given the abbreviated development time for the B-24, which first flew on December 29, 1939—more than four years after the first B-17 variant took wing. NARA

Pre-Combat Liberators

The XB-24 first tested its graceful Davis wing on December 29, 1939, using parts borrowed from another Consolidated Aircraft prototype, the Model 31 flying boat, to make that very first B-24 flight a day under nine months from the signing of the contract that authorized its design and construction. In a fitting irony, the very existence of the B-24 resulted from Consolidated's response to an Air Corps query about building B-17s under license.[9]

At the same time B-24s were being developed for the Army Air Forces, Liberators were being built for the Royal Air Force. The AAF's lone YB-24 and few B-24A versions were similar in appearance and equipment to the original XB-24 and roughly followed the form of the Royal Air Force Liberator I. The sole XB-24B was the rejuvenated XB-24, a test bed for a number of improvements including the wide oval engine nacelles that became a B-24 hallmark. In the process, the original XB-24 serial number (39-556) was retired and replaced with the XB-24B's serial, 39-680.[10]

The export British Liberator II introduced a nose section lengthened by about three feet, which forever transformed subsequent variants that were not as pug-nosed as the first Liberators. When the AAF took delivery of nine B-24Cs, they appeared very much as the follow-on D-model would, with the longer nose and a newly installed Martin upper-power turret located just aft of the cockpit.

The 389th Bomb Group's *Missouri Mauler*, a B-24D from Convair's Fort Worth plant, flies between two cloud decks. The dulled national insignia seems to be thwarted by the bright white disc on the tail. Second Air Division

When unique markings were desired for formation ships to enable groups to form up for the outbound flight, the Liberator groups took full artistic license in devising unmistakable paint schemes, like the white front end with red and black polka dots on this 458th Bomb Group example. After rallying its group's bombers in formation, the formation ship, typically no longer combat-worthy, would return to its base. USAFA/Brown/Olmsted

Patches and scars on the fuselage of *Mountain Time* attest to rugged use of this Ford Liberator, possibly part of the 487th Bomb Group. Cockpit armor and bulging navigator's "basket" window were add-ons. USAFA/Brown

The ball turret gunner had this view of his confined capsule upon entry. Black box is the K-4 computing gunsight. Immediately above the box in the picture are portions of the two handgrips that served to traverse and elevate the turret. This is an A-13 retractable turret in a B-24. Convair/SDAM

The first mass-production AAF B-24 to see combat was the D-model, which reached Eighth Air Force in late 1942. With a listed gross weight of 60,000 pounds, the B-24D was capable of carrying up to 8,800 pounds of bombs—but bomb load and range were the perpetual tradeoff of any aircraft. It cruised at 200 miles per hour and had a top speed of 303 miles per hour at 25,000 feet.

The B-24D relied on four Pratt and Whitney R1830-43 radial engines, each rated at 1,200 horsepower. For armament, a Consolidated-designed hydraulic-powered tail turret carried two .50-caliber machine guns. A Martin electrically driven top turret carried two more .50-calibers. Ventral protection of D-model Liberators was variously handled by a Bendix remotely sighted power turret that was discontinued and ultimately replaced by a retractable version of the manned Sperry lower ball turret that had proven successful on the B-17. Some B-24Ds used a single handheld .50-caliber weapon in a truss that swung into the rear ventral hatch instead of any power turret. The superior Sperry ball turret made its debut on B-24D-CO number 42-41164. A number of B-24Ds assigned to the Eighth Air Force predated the introduction of the lower ball turret and had only the single tunnel gun for ventral protection. (Later, in 1944, ball turrets were taken out of a number of Eighth Air Force B-24s of later models as a way to improve performance of the increasingly encumbered bombers.) B-24D production totaled 2,728 aircraft, some of which were dispatched all over the world to conduct America's global air war.

Into Battle with the B-24D

Eighth Air Force B-24D Liberators carried evolving markings on their increasingly battle-scarred hides as 1943 progressed. Aircraft number 42-40619 of the 389th Bomb Group shows the geometric Circle-C group identifier on the outside of its vertical fins and on the upper right wing surface, as instated by VIII Bomber Command beginning in June 1943. The national insignia shows evidence of gray over the white star and bars to diminish visibility, surrounded by a red outline briefly prescribed in the summer of 1943. In the hectic pace of war, emblem changes may sometimes have lagged behind directives. USAF photo

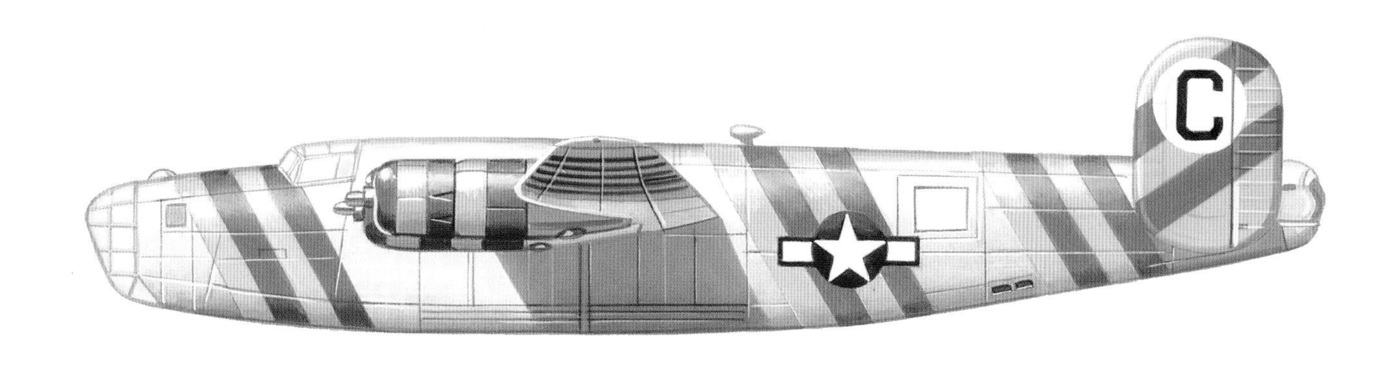

GREEN DRAGON, 389th Bomb Group

Hoopoe, an early Convair Fort Worth B-24D (42-63779), carried an Eighth Air Force emblem on its nose when photographed tipped back on a snowy field. Some B-24s carried a small stand to be placed beneath the tail skid and under the aft fuselage to preclude this from happening. This D-model may later have been converted by Eighth Air Force to nominal C-87 Liberator Express configuration.

The early Consolidated power tail turret, while a mechanical marvel in its time, was still a drafty place to fight a war at 25,000 feet. The flat pane between the guns was laminated safety glass that gave the gunner a measure of protection from gunfire. To accommodate ammunition feedways, early turrets staggered the two machine guns, with the turret's left gun protruding out farther than the right. Beveled muzzle-blast deflectors helped direct blast away from the other barrel. The demarcation point for the gray and olive paint on the rudder coincided with the elevator. Convair photo

Late in the combat career of the 489th Bomb Group's 845th Bomb Squadron, *The Sharon D.* received a solid yellow tail under the auspices of the 20th Composite Wing. Unpainted (or possibly aluminum-silver painted) armor has been mounted outside the cockpit, touching the edges of the nickname lettering. The photo dates to October 1944 at Halesworth. Jim Kiernan and Sharon D. Vance Kiernan

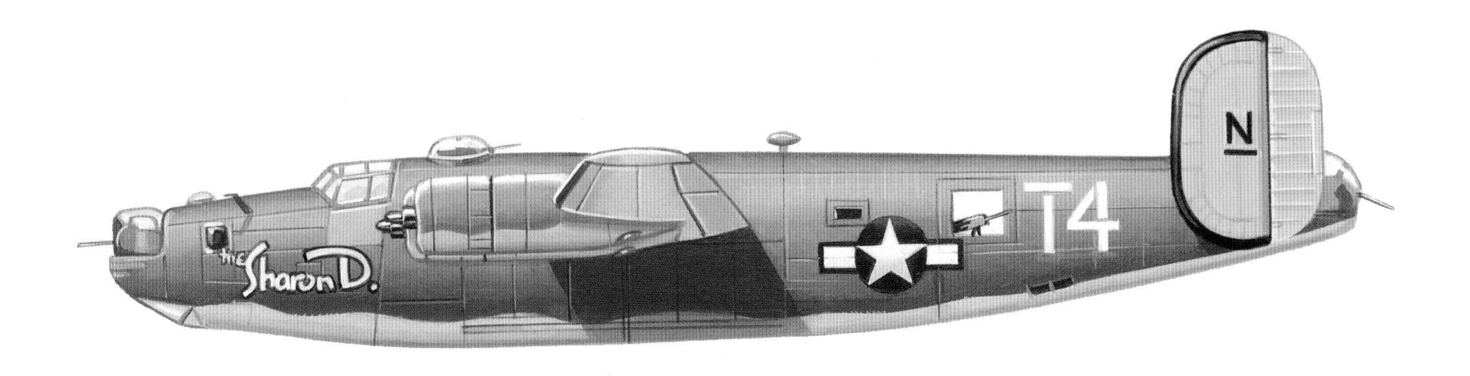

SHARON D.

B-24H and B-24J

The experience of the Ford Motor Company in building Liberator bombers at its immense Willow Run plant in Michigan can be characterized as one of learning with the B-24E and attaining operational capability with the B-24H. The Ford E-model was, at least superficially, a copy of Convair's greenhouse-nose B-24D. Ford personnel learned it was a far different proposition to build a heavy bomber from aluminum than it was to manufacture thousands of automobiles from steel, and the Army Air Forces realized Ford needed to use its production of B-24Es as a teaching tool. E-models were built with fewer changes during the course of production than some variants. While this allowed Ford to concentrate on the nuances of perfecting bomber construction, it also resulted in a production run that was already deemed unsuitable for the evolving combat by the time they were finished. B-24Es typically filled training and miscellaneous duties at home. The first production Liberator to carry a power nose turret, early Ford-built H-models were dispatched to the Eighth Air Force's 392nd Bomb Group. The Emerson A-15 electrically driven nose turret added about a foot in length to the B-24H over the D-model. As with all nose-turreted Liberators in combat, the bombardier's working space was cramped by the addition of a turret in the upper nose.

Ford's nose turret installation used a sheet-metal fairing and a bombardier's window arrangement unlike those employed by Convair and North American at their Liberator assembly lines. By virtue of knock-down kits made by Ford and sent to Douglas in Tulsa, Oklahoma, and Convair in Fort Worth (until home-grown production took over at Fort Worth), some nose-turreted B-24s assembled in Tulsa and Fort Worth have the characteristics of a Ford nose. Production of B-24Hs at Willow Run, Tulsa, and Fort Worth totaled 3,100 aircraft.

The Convair San Diego plant went directly from B-24D production to building B-24Js with nose turrets. Many similarities make it difficult to discern some B-24Hs from J-models. San Diego J-models from Blocks 1 through 180 used versions of the Consolidated A6A and A6B hydraulic nose turret. These turrets are distinguishable from Emerson turrets by the angled armor glass used in the Consolidated design. Some Fort Worth J-models also used sloping A6 nose turrets before all Liberator assembly lines standardized on the cylindrical Emerson A-15 turret. B-24 production hit its high with the J-model, the only model produced on all five assembly lines, for a total of 6,678 aircraft.

Eighth Air Force units operated B-24Hs from Ford, Douglas, and Convair Fort Worth, and J-models from Ford, Douglas, North American, Convair San Diego and Fort Worth.

Leon Vance and daughter Sharon Drury Vance posed beside her B-24H namesake, *The Sharon D.*, before the 489th Bomb Group flew to England in the spring of 1944. Jim Kiernan and Sharon D. Vance Kiernan

A 93rd Bomb Group Ford B-24H provided a topic for an AAF photographer to study between missions. But a bomber on the ramp was not winning the war, so throughout the fight the Eighth Air Force honed its radar bombing skills to enable more missions to be completed in spite of inclement weather over Germany. Jerry Cole collection

***Gashouse Gus* is likely a Convair Fort Worth–assembled B-24H, using a Ford kit. The nose is Ford-style; the straight camouflage demarcation line between olive and gray is typical of Convair.** USAFA/Brown

Bright white and black tail plus fuselage letters EC identify an early Ford B-24H (42-7478) from the 392nd Bomb Group's 578th Bomb Squadron. With the adoption of such brightly painted outer vertical tail surfaces on Eighth Air Force B-24s beginning around April 1944, serial numbers often were relocated to the inside surfaces of the vertical fins where they were still readily visible. The bright colors, arranged in patterns unique to each bomb group, were adopted in an effort to make it easier for hundreds of Eighth Air Force warplanes to sort themselves out while forming up and to ensure proper placement of groups. AAF/NARA

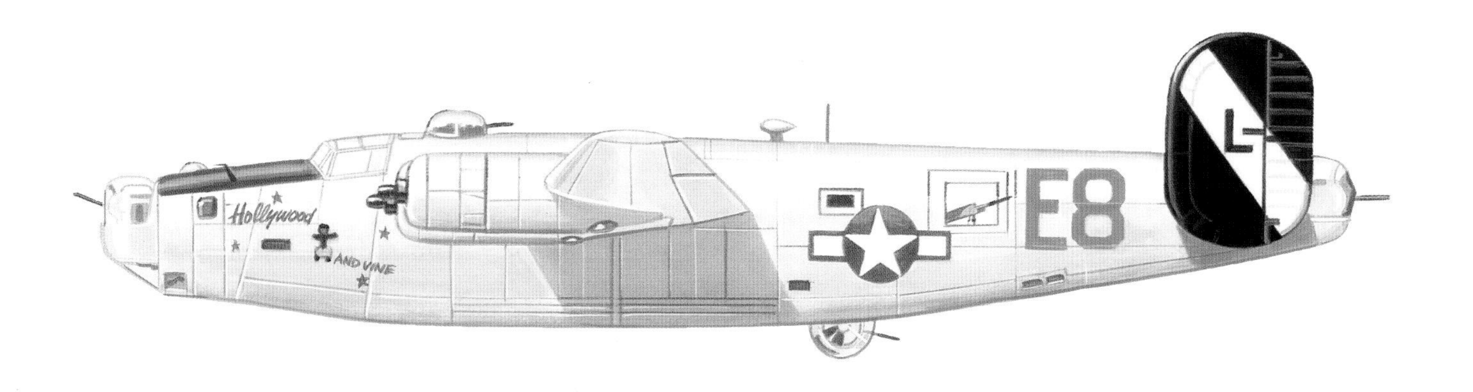

HOLLYWOOD & VINE, 734th Bomb Squadron/453rd Bomb Group

An oft-repeated pin-up pose adorned the 446th Bomb Group's *Shoo Shoo Baby,* a B-24H-FO (42-52747). By the time of this color photo, the B-24 may have been repaired from chin damage apparent in other photos of it; new skin appears to overlay the bottom of the letters in the first part of *Baby.* Ford pioneered the use of outward-opening B-24 nosewheel doors; Convair followed suit. Krassman/Ethell

Bright ornamentation highlighted *The Joker,* a Convair San Diego B-24J (44-40472). The fire extinguisher door on the left side of the nose was painted red at the factory. The curved black line near the nosewheel opening is a snubber line; when viewed from ahead of the Liberator by a tug driver, lines on either side of the nose provided a reference to how sharply the nosewheel could be turned to either side. USAFA/Brown

TUBARAO, 491st Bomb Group

Responding to complaints about lack of visibility from the noses of turret-equipped Liberators, Eighth Air Force installed so-called basket windows that bulged out to provide a greater field of vision for navigators and bombardiers. The installation and touch-up painting partially obliterated the *Shady Lady* nickname on this Convair B-24J (44-40439). USAFA/Brown

Sun angle helps define the high camber over the top of the B-24's Davis high-lift wing design. Black Circle-J denotes an aircraft from the 453rd Bomb Group as it passes over the target area where puffs of smoke show the bombing pattern. Al Lloyd collection

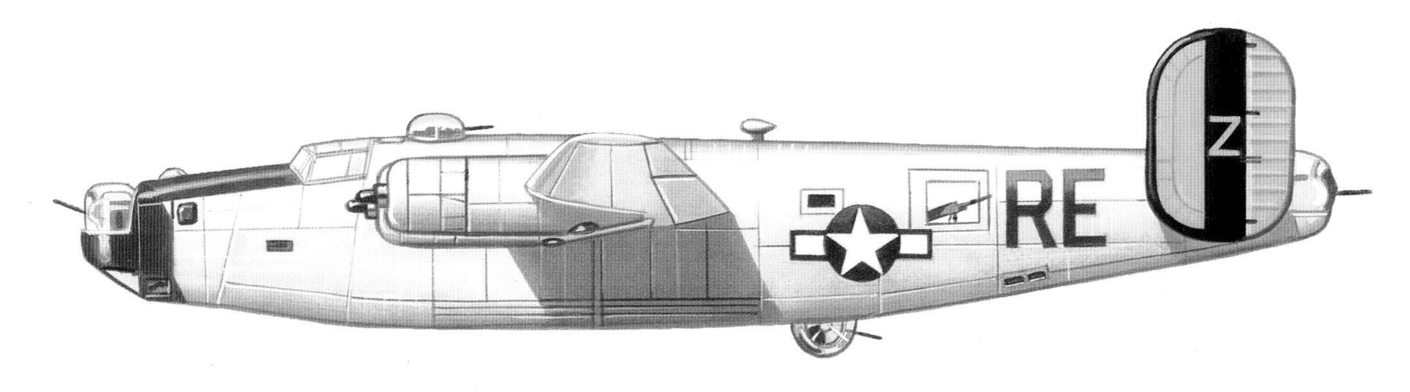

B-24H PATHFINDER, 93rd BOMB GROUP

Bonnie B, a B-24J (44-40378) built in San Diego served with the 493rd Bomb Group until that unit converted to B-17Gs in September 1944. Traits identifying this as a San Diego Liberator include the shape of the anti-glare panel ahead of the windshield, curved to intersect the astrodome. The use of a Motor Products variant of the Consolidated nose turret is another San Diego practice, until later Liberator production standardized the cylindrical Emerson electric nose turret. Framing around the canopy shows evidence of thick bullet-resistant glass that the Eighth Air Force used on some B-24s as well as B-17s. USAFA/Brown

Published in *National Geographic* magazine during the war, this Army Air Forces Kodachrome documented how crews learned to compensate when brakes were shot out by securing parachutes to be tossed from the waist windows during rollout. Some red pigments are prone to fading; the tail of this 466th Bomb Group Douglas Tulsa B-24H (42-51141) shows streaks. USAF

A thick plume of smoke issuing from a lone Liberator far below the formation does not bode well as a drama plays out in contested skies over Europe. Second Air Division

Lettering on the B-24 nicknamed *Call Me "Savage"* appears to have been reiterated after bolt-on armor was added beside the co-pilot's station. USAFA/Brown

B-24D-CO (42-40990) *On The Ball* of the 93rd Bomb Group (identified by the Circle-B on the tail) presented a generally dull appearance when photographed in 1943, after the toned-down national insignia incorporated side bars and a red surround that was mandated that June. Jerry Cole collection

Rush hour, Eighth Air Force style, saw a line of 458th Bomb Group B-24s ready for a mission on Christmas Eve, 1944, because the war did not take holidays. AAF

B-24L and B24M

Ford developed a prodigious capacity for Liberator production. By mid-1944, Ford and Convair San Diego could meet ongoing Liberator production demands, so the other assembly lines could convert to different wartime urgencies. Only San Diego and Willow Run built the last two B-24 variants mass-produced, the B-24L and M-models.

Convair began enclosing waist windows on L-models, something Ford had done during the production of B-24Hs. A variety of other changes, characterized by the introduction of a lightweight tail-gun enclosure with narrowly spaced twin .50-caliber machine guns, attended production of B-24Ls. When the last B-24L was delivered, 1,667 of this model had been built.

The ultimate production Liberator, the B-24M, saw the evolution of waist guns to include K-7 mounts accommodating K-13 computing gunsights. Block-20 Ford B-24Ms introduced a completely redesigned cockpit canopy shape with fewer metal ribs and opening overhead escape hatches. B-24M production totaled 2,593 Liberators. An abundance of photographic evidence suggests that a number of Ford M-models reached Eighth Air Force; Convair B-24Ms may have been more prevalent in the Pacific.

A 493rd Bomb Group crew suits up for a B-24 mission circa June 1944. In their pile of gear are a number of regular G.I. army helmets worn by some aircrew members instead of purpose-made flak helmets. USAFA/Brown collection

Bombing Through Overcast

As Eighth Air Force expanded its complement of radar-equipped Pathfinder aircraft to enable formations to bomb through overcast conditions, both B-17s and, later, B-24s were fitted with radar. The first four B-24s from Eighth Air Force to see combat as Pathfinders participated in missions on January 11, 1944, against a cluster of industrial targets in Germany. On the 28th of that month, a force of 43 Eighth Air Force B-24s bombed a V-weapon site at Bonnieres, France, using a different blind-bombing aid, Gee-H, for the first time. Unlike H2X radar, Gee-H relied on a transmitted beacon with a maximum range of 200 miles from the beacon station. Though considered more accurate than onboard radar, the limiting range of Gee-H was an issue.[11]

This well-dappled B-24D is probably 44th Bomb Group's *Lemon Drop* early in its career. *Lemon Drop* later became the assembly ship used to help the rest of the 44th Bomb Group form up for a mission. NARA

Colors were reversed when painting geometric symbols with letters on silver aircraft instead of olive-drab bombers. Here the Square-X identifies the 493rd Bomb Group.
USAFA/Brown

***Sugar Baby* of the 446th Bomb Group was a patchwork of colors in early 1945. Yellow edging on bomb bay doors was used on some Eighth Air Force B-24s as a cue to the position of the roll-up doors. The aft door, evidently cannibalized from an older Liberator, carries dark gray camouflage paint.**
Krassman/Ethell/Lloyd

New pavement and freshly tilled earth form the home f the 493rd Bomb Group's B-24s at Debach in the summer of 1944. The 493rd was the last Eighth Air Force group to become operational, on the auspicious date of June 6, 1944.
USAFA/Brown

A natural metal Convair B-24 follows a camouflaged Ford Liberator as the 493rd Bomb Group goes to war in the summer of 1944. USAFA/Brown

The word picture on this Ford Liberator in England is *Feather Merchant.* Even spacing of demarcation scallops between gray and olive drab is evident in this color view. USAFA/Brown

Taxiing 493rd Bomb Group B-24s include the ill-fated *Little Warrior,* middle left, that was later photographed burning fiercely after a flak hit during a mission to Quakenbruk on June 29, 1944. **(see photo, p. 50)**
USAFA/Brown

Eighth Air Force B-24 markings generally followed the pattern of B-17s. Early B-24Ds sometimes were blotched with medium green to break up the angularity of the olive drab on wings and tail surfaces. Later camouflaged Liberators, like their B-17 counterparts, often were not dappled with green blotching. Some Eighth Air Force B-24 white star insignia were subdued with gray to diminish their brilliance from a distance, a practice that still prevailed, seemingly incongruously, on some natural-metal Eighth Air Force B-24s.

A Bomb Group letter contained in a disc or square on the vertical tails and upper right wing surfaces was complemented by the standardized squadron and individual aircraft letters on the fuselages of Eighth Air Force Liberators. By October 1943, camouflage for AAF aircraft including B-24s was no longer mandatory, and the following year saw a major influx of natural metal finish Liberators into the Eighth Air Force.

A unique marking seen on some Eighth Air Force B-24s is yellow striping on the edges of the bomb bay doors where they meet in the middle of the bomb bay. When rolled open up the fuselage sides, these yellow marks provided a reference that the flush doors were open—unlike a B-17, whose bomb doors hinged into the slipstream as a clear giveaway that they were open, B-24 doors were more difficult to detect.

A tanker truck replenishes the Eighth Air Force B-24 *Snafuperman* to help get it ready for the next mission.
Brown collection

P-38 Lightning

This Lockheed photo shows the unusual planform of the large twin-engine Lightning. This example is a P-38J (42-68008).

The large yet graceful twin-engine Lockheed P-38 Lightning fighter was prime for combat over Europe as part of early Eighth Air Force efforts. Its ability to carry two 150-gallon or 300-gallon drop tanks made it a natural for long-range escort duties at a time when both the P-47 and P-51 were still in development. As the Eighth Air Force coalesced in 1942, only the P-38 was ready to escort bombers over Europe along with British Spitfires.

The Lockheed P-38 Lightning was an innovative response to a 1937 Army Air Corps specification calling for a pursuit plane that could attain 360 miles per hour at 20,000 feet. In the pre-war period, maneuverable fighters were not prized yet as long-range bomber escorts, and the P-38's original role was to challenge offensive enemy aircraft as a pursuit. A deep suspicion of Army ground commanders permeated Air Corps planning, and initially pursuit aircraft were deliberately built without a capacity to carry range-extending droppable fuel tanks, lest this feature be converted to make fighters into *de facto* bombers to support troops on the ground. The Air Corps coveted independence and the ability to apply its assets in a unified manner, and the specter of turning fighters into close-support aircraft threatened this unity and autonomy.[1]

The first flight of the sleek XP-38 on January 27, 1939, in California showed the gleaming silver prototype to be a harbinger of a new age in fighter aircraft. When the prototype crashed two weeks later at the end of a transcontinental flight, the loss did not close down the fledgling program. The follow-on baker's dozen YP-38 models continued to prove the concept, and P-38 production moved model-by-model ever closer to the operational Lightnings that first faced the Axis in 1942. Even as early combat by European fighters pointed the way toward P-38 improvements like self-sealing gas tanks and armor glass windscreens, the Lightning reached a level of operational sufficiency by the advent of the P-38E in 1941.

The prohibition against external shackles on Air Corps fighters was revisited in 1941, and the P-38F was the first model fitted with drop tanks to extend its range. Still, the original reasoning behind adapting the P-38 to carry external gasoline tanks was not to enable its use as a long-range bomber escort. In 1940, the Air Corps sent officer Benjamin S. Kelsey to Europe to study the aerial combat then raging between Germany and its neighbors. Kelsey concluded that the fall of France and the serious threat Germany posed to Allied convoys could make it imperative to ferry fighters to England; hence, the requirement for extra fuel tanks.[2]

During F-model production, a change to the wing flaps beginning with Block-15 aircraft allowed the flaps to be partially extended at combat speeds not exceeding 250 miles per hour, resulting in increased lift and maneuverability. Equipment variations resulted in the designation P-38G. By May 1943, the P-38H, with its ability to carry heavier underwing loads, was in service.

The P-38J defined later Lightning production with its introduction of noticeably deeper chin radiator contours than used on previous models. Later J-models had increased internal fuel capacity. With the added range provided by a pair of 300-gallon drop tanks, the P-38J had a combat radius sufficient to penetrate deep into Germany on bomber escort missions. The P-38L used 1,600-horsepower Allison engines but was otherwise similar to the J-model.

A generic Lockheed P-38L cockpit shows the Lightning's unique bow-tie control wheel, unusual for a fighter. This wheel incorporated the basics of two fighter stick grips. Peter M. Bowers collection

The 1st Fighter Group flew olive-drab P-38F Lightnings to England in June and July 1942. Their introduction to combat was delayed as they were fitted with British-style VHF (Very High Frequency) radios instead of the shorter-range HF (High Frequency) sets common in AAF aircraft of that period. The first AAF aerial victory in the European Theater of Operations (ETO) was a shared kill, with an Iceland-based P-39 Airacobra and a 1st Fighter Group P-38F downing a Focke Wulf Fw-200 Kondor four-engine patrol bomber off the coast of Iceland on August 14. The Lightning was part of the 27th Fighter Squadron from the 1st Group that worked out of Iceland temporarily, flying defensive patrols.

On August 29, 1942, two pairs of P-38s from the 1st Group went looking for action in the face of enemy aircraft reported approaching the coast, but no contact was made. By September 26, Lightnings were launched on escort duty for B-17s, but poor weather necessitated aborting the mission. Then, on October 9, 1942, the 1st Fighter Group sent 36 P-38s to escort B-17s and, in their combat debut for the Eighth, B-24Ds of the 93rd Bomb Group, as the bombers reached targets at Lille, France.

At the factory, Lockheed workers service a new P-38. Smudges around the nose imply the guns have already been tested in the firing butt. Lockheed photo

P-38J

LUCKY LADY (Arthur Heiden), 79th Fighter Squadron/20th Fighter Group

In the fall of 1942, some P-38 pilots, including Eighth Air Force fliers, found themselves in high-speed dives during which the elevators became ineffectual. The little-understood phenomenon of compressibility rendered the Lightnings—and other fighters—plummeting sleds until lower altitudes and denser air made recovery sometimes possible. Changes ultimately applied to the P-38 included dive flaps on the lower surface of the wings that could alter aerodynamic traits enough to thwart compressibility.

Soon the 14th Fighter Group P-38s bolstered the Eighth Air Force. But even as Eighth Air Force strength grew, it was hemorrhaging as the needs of North Africa prompted the AAF to reassign units, including P-38 groups, to Twelfth Air Force in September and October 1942. The largely unproven concept of daylight heavy bombardment from English bases was a less powerful argument in 1942 than were the needs of Allied forces being groomed for battle in North Africa. Eighth Air Force would give up three early P-38 units, the 1st, 14th, and 82nd Fighter Groups, to the new Twelfth Air Force in North Africa in late 1942.

The answer to high-speed compressibility dives in the P-38 was to deploy dive flaps attached beneath the wing to alter the airflow and retain controllability of the Lightning. Author photo

Other units would bring more Lightnings to the Eighth Air Force later in 1943. Combined factors, ranging from securing Atlantic convoy sea lanes to increased American production, led to more inventory arriving in England for the use of Eighth Air Force as 1943 aged on the calendar. The 55th Fighter Group flew P-38Hs into combat starting October 15, 1943, becoming the first fully operational Lightning group in the Eighth. The 55th Fight Group switched to P-38Js by the end of December. Their J-model Lightnings were replaced by P-51 Mustangs during July 1944. To the P-38s of the 55th goes the unique honor of being the first Eighth Air Force warplanes over Berlin, escorting a bombing mission there on March 3, 1944.[3]

The 20th Fighter Group flew P-38Hs and P-38Js, seeing first combat three days after Christmas 1943. They turned in the last of their P-38s for Mustangs late in July 1944. While flying Lightnings, the 20th Group earned a Distinguished Unit Citation for a sweep over Germany flown on April 8, 1944.[4]

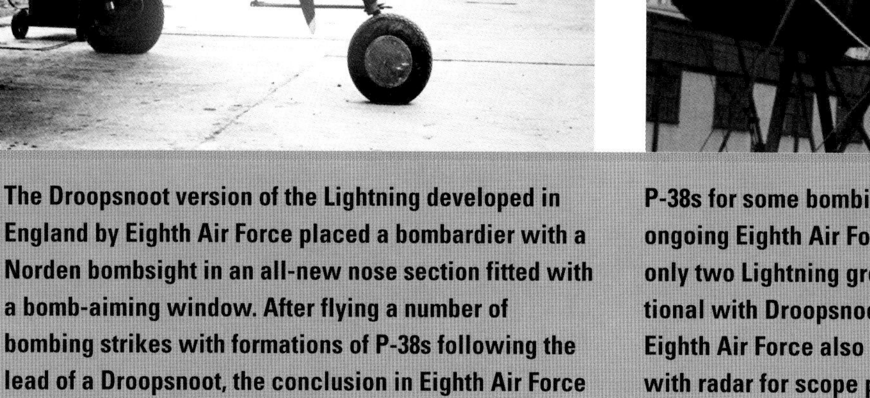

The Droopsnoot version of the Lightning developed in England by Eighth Air Force placed a bombardier with a Norden bombsight in an all-new nose section fitted with a bomb-aiming window. After flying a number of bombing strikes with formations of P-38s following the lead of a Droopsnoot, the conclusion in Eighth Air Force was that traditional bombers could accomplish this task. Initially, there seemed to be an economy in using P-38s for some bombing missions. As a result of the ongoing Eighth Air Force fighter conversion to P-51s, only two Lightning groups in England became operational with Droopsnoot lead aircraft in time to try it. Eighth Air Force also tested a Droopsnoot P-38 fitted with radar for scope photography, but limitations inherent in the radar installation in the P-38 airframe limited the field of coverage available. AAF

MY DAD [James M. Morris], 20th Fighter Group/77th Fighter Squadron

Upper right, opposite page: Not all P-38s flew the Atlantic; deck passage brought Lightnings wrapped for protection against the salty sea environment. SAF/SDAM

P-38Gs of the 78th Fighter Group never saw combat with the Eighth Air Force before being replaced by P-47Cs in early 1943. Nonetheless, the 78th became the only Eighth Air Force fighter group to have flown all three types of escort fighters used by the AAF in England: P-38s, P-47s, and P-51s.

The 364th Fighter Group began Eighth Air Force combat with P-38s in March 1944, switching to P-51s by that summer. Similarly, the 479th Fighter Group used its P-38s for Eighth Air Force fighter escort from May 1944, converting to Mustangs around September of that year, and bringing Eighth Air Force Lightning escort operations to a close.

The combat history of the Lightning in Eighth Air Force was truncated by the removal of early groups to Twelfth Air Force, and the 1944 conversion of later P-38 groups in England to P-47s and P-51s. At the direction of General Dwight Eisenhower, who was crafting plans for fighting in North Africa in 1942, Eighth Air Force was required to give up two P-38 fighter groups to the North African campaign. Historian Richard G. Davis' detailed account of AAF General Carl A. Spaatz discusses a decision between Spaatz and Hap Arnold, made during a meeting in North Africa in January 1943, to furnish fighter units in England solely with P-47s.[5] This was before the debut of the Merlin-engine P-51B Mustang. Later, Eighth Air Force's James Doolittle was said to favor a streamlined force structure of B-17s and P-51s. It is easier to maintain supply lines when fewer aircraft types must be cared for at far-flung bases. If Doolittle's preference for Mustangs over Lightnings frustrated staunch P-38 proponents like Lockheed test pilot and technical representative Tony LeVier, there was nonetheless a valid logistical reason for winnowing Eighth Air Force fighters down to one type whenever possible.

Lockheed dispatched LeVier to England early in 1944 to help Eighth Air Force P-38 pilots get the most out of their Lightnings. Compressibility dive worries and engine failures vied for attention as the demons LeVier needed to exorcise. A veteran of both events, LeVier showed P-38 pilots how he could make single-engine takeoffs, and maneuver with turns into the dead engine—a new pilot's nightmare because it can aggravate stall characteristics on many airplanes. Before he returned to the United States, Tony LeVier created a manual for Eighth Air Force P-38 fliers to teach them how to get longer range from their fighters by careful management of their Allison engines.[6]

LeVier and Lockheed engineer Ward Beman told Eighth Air Force Lightning pilots how to recover from the grip of compressibility in dives by maintaining enough

O.D. and Silver

Olive and gray Eighth Air Force P-38 belonged to the 55th Fighter Group's 338th Fighter Squadron. The letters CL on the boom and the disc on its tail were squadron indicators. Though Lockheed's representative in England, Tony LeVier, believed the P-38 could surmount some engine and compressibility issues, the Lightning was not to become an Eighth Air Force mainstay. AFHRA

P-38s began serving Eighth Air Force in olive drab and gray camouflage. By the end of Eighth Air Force service in August 1944, Lightnings in the 479th Fighter Group were natural metal with colored rudders denoting squadrons. Lightnings of the 7th Photo Group also were natural metal finish by this time, replacing the photo reconnaissance blue that was previously sprayed on the F-4 and F-5 Lightnings they operated.

At one point, olive drab Eighth Air Force Lightnings used white geometric shapes—a circular disk, square box, or triangle—in white on the outer surfaces of both vertical fins as squadron recognition features, with coded letters on the tail booms identifying specific groups and squadrons. The unique twin-boom planform of the Lockheed P-38 was easy to distinguish from any other aircraft. Therefore, Eighth Air Force P-38s did not sport the recognition bands that were applied to P-47s and P-51s to distinguish them from similar German fighters.

back pressure on the P-38's control yoke to induce at least moderate buffeting, while making very small up-elevator trim tab inputs. Too much backpressure and trim could break the tail booms just ahead of the horizontal stabilizer. Part of a successful recovery from a high-speed dive demanded the fortitude to simply ride the plane down into denser air.

As soon as LeVier got his hands on a dive flap–equipped P-38J, he was able to dispel remaining doubts about P-38 dive recoverability. By operating the dive flaps early in a dive, it was possible to maintain control of the Lightning more easily than without the addition of the underwing dive flaps.[7]

In retrospect, the P-38 Lightning may have suffered for being the AAF's only multi-engine day fighter. It was somewhat of a curiosity, bound to be compared with the mundane German ME-110 twin-engine fighter, even though the P-38 was a superior performer. The challenges of compressibility were not unique to the P-38, although some spectacular and widely witnessed P-38 crashes out of dives may have given the Lightning a bum rap for compressibility problems. And the engine failures, which Tony LeVier believed he put to rest in England, were a phenomenon seemingly aggravated by the combination of cold and humidity found at altitude in the European Theater of Operations.

There is another facet to the tale of the Lightning in England that P-38 proponents look upon as a lost opportunity. In 1942 and well into 1943, only the P-38 had the range to protect B-17 and B-24 formations deep inside

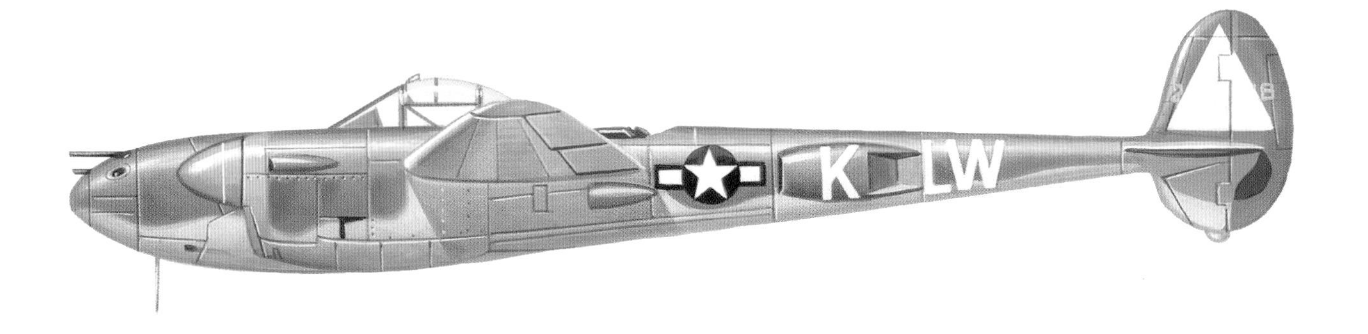

P-38L, 55th Fighter Squadron/20th Fighter Group

A silver Lockheed P-38 Lightning wears a black square geometric shape on its tail, identifying the fighter as part of the 364th Fighter Group. This unit converted to P-51s in the summer of 1944, as P-38s were removed from the Eighth Air Force in favor of P-51s. Photo via 91st Bomb Group reunion

Germany. But for reasons that probably included a dose of AAF narcissism early in the war, the value of long-range escort fighters still was not fully appreciated by decision-makers. The unusual P-38, with its two engines, tricycle landing gear, and control wheel instead of a joystick, didn't fit the norm for a fighter. While duplicate production lines were established for both P-47s and P-51s, Lightnings would only issue from Lockheed at Burbank. By war's end, the P-38's most illustrious combat achievements would be recorded in the Pacific, not over Fortress Europe.

As Eighth Air Force scrambled to give its heavy bombers longer-ranging fighter escorts, P-38s reached out from a range of 520 miles, which they achieved by November 1943, to 585 miles by the following February. Though they could range farther into Germany than the beefy P-47s, Lightnings would still ultimately be bested in range by single-engine P-51 Mustangs in the ETO.

On November 13, 1943, the longest Eighth Air Force escort mission to date was accomplished when 45 of 48 dispatched P-38s stayed with the bombers all the way to Bremen, Germany. Seven Lightnings were lost, five of them were to German fighters. The momentum was building as more Eighth Air Force bombers and fighters kept inviting themselves into German airspace.[8]

CHAPTER 5

P-47 Thunderbolt

A P-47D (42-26243) of the 56th Fighter Group shows the silver cockpit canopy that was typical of the group's camouflaged Thunderbolts, both razorbacks and bubble tops. Absent are the identification stripes on the tail that had earlier characterized P-47s in England. USAFA/Brown

It towered over contemporaries, a hulking airframe pulled through the skies by a massive air-cooled radial engine. The size of the P-47 enabled it to pack more firepower, with eight .50-caliber machine guns nested in its wings, than other American fighters. It was fast and could carry drop tanks to Germany. It was a contender, an ace-maker.

Designers at Republic (earlier Seversky) Aircraft on Long Island had an affinity for stocky radial-engine fighters. The Seversky P-35 introduced retractable landing gear to single-seat Air Corps fighters in 1936. Evolutionary XP-41 and P-43 designs melded a turbosupercharger in the aft fuselage of designs that bear unmistakable traits of the later, and resoundingly successful, P-47 Thunderbolt.

The Thunderbolt came about after Republic engineers discarded a couple of paper designs under the designations XP-47 and XP-47A that were intended for the Allison V-1710 inline engine, as used on the P-38 and early P-51s. The first aircraft to fly as a P-47 was the prototype XP-47B, a giant silver wonder that initially became airborne on May 6, 1941. The XP-47B was clocked at 412 miles per hour at 25,800 feet; later Thunderbolts would nudge that top speed and altitude higher.

Colonel Francis S. Gabreski ran his tally of P-47 victories up to 28 aircraft while flying with the Eighth Air Force's 56th Fighter Group. AAF

Four side-by-side tracks of .50-caliber machine gun ammunition in the wings of Thunderbolts necessitated staggering the guns for ease of feeding. Armorers were photographed carefully loading a victory-emblazoned bubble-canopy P-47D. AFHRA

Red-cowled Thunderbolts of the 63rd Fighter Squadron are in position on the Boxted runway. The 56th Fighter Group from which these P-47s came remained true to the Thunderbolt, while other units switched to P-51s. USAFA/Brown

Production P-47Bs resembled the prototype, although they introduced a sliding canopy instead of the XP-47B's hinged panels. The first combat variant of the Thunderbolt was the C-model, capable of carrying a 200-gallon centerline fuel tank beneath its fuselage. A 13-inch fuselage stretch, including an 8-inch extension of the motor mounts, improved the C-model's center of gravity. Of 602 P-47Cs built, a number were sent to the Eighth Air Force.

The signature variant of the Thunderbolt was the P-47D. Curiously, while the D-model underwent a major alteration during production with the substitution of a bubble canopy for the earlier razorback design, no new model letter was assigned, so P-47Ds can be either razorbacks or bubble tops. The use of R-2800-59 engines with water injection gave the P-47D a speed of better than 430 miles per hour. Also introduced during the production run of D-models were underwing pylons enabling the use of more drop tanks or bombs. Even as bombers swapped narrow "toothpick" propeller blades for wider paddles that gave better high-altitude performance, so did the P-47D adopt wider prop blades during production. With the help of an additional P-47 assembly line in Evansville, Indiana, production of P-47Ds totaled 6,315 fighters.

Subsequent model letters E and F were given to experimental Thunderbolts testing a pressurized cockpit and laminar flow wings, respectively. The 354 P-47Gs were similar to D-models but were produced under contract by Curtiss-Wright. The XP-47Hs tested an experimental Chrysler engine; the letter I was not assigned to avoid confusion with the number 1. The J-model Thunderbolt was a single test bed that Republic said flew faster than 500 miles per hour. The XP-47K was a test bed that introduced the bubble canopy used on the D-model in July 1943, while the XP-47L tanked more gasoline in the fuselage than a standard D-model.

The last Thunderbolts to see combat with Eighth Air Force were among the 130 P-47Ms that roared at 470 miles per hour at 30,000 feet as an interim answer to the threat of faster German jets and buzz bombs. The speedy M-models incorporated Dash-57 engines with CH-5 turbosuperchargers.

Accounts vary on the first operational use of Eighth Air Force Thunderbolts. A March 10, 1943, fighter sweep by 14 P-47s of the 4th Fighter Group would have become historic had the American fighters encountered their German adversaries. As it turned out, it was fortunate

The hefty P-47C (41-6630) *Spokane Chief* surrounds pilot Major Eugene Roberts in the cockpit. This early 78th Fighter Group Thunderbolt carried three victory crosses when the photo was taken; by August 31, 1943, Major Roberts was a five-victory ace on his way to a wartime Eighth Air Force total of nine. *Spokane Chief* artwork appeared on both sides of the fuselage. A rearview mirror is built into the top of the windshield frame to enable the pilot to "check six" (meaning, to watch the position directly behind his fighter, compared to the six position on a clock face) to avoid the enemy. AAF/NARA

The 56th Fighter Group's *Bonnie* and pilot paused for an informal portrait at Boxted in the summer of 1944. This razorback P-47D is fitted with a Hamilton-Standard propeller, as evidenced by the bluntly rounded silver prop hub; other P-47Ds in the unit at the same time flew with Curtiss Electric propellers, characterized by longer, less rounded hub covers. USAFA/Brown

Decorated bubble top and razorback P-47Ds of the 56th Fighter Group are ready to launch in England circa July 1944. Open cowl flaps at rear edge of engine cowlings allow more prop wash to rush past the finned cylinders of the P-47s' air-cooled engines during ground runs, when overheating is a danger. USAFA/Brown

Some silver P-47s were later camouflaged in Europe. This P-47D's identification letters, HV*Z, mark it as part of the 56th Fighter Group's 61st Fighter Squadron. The over-painted portion of the top right corner of the letter "Z" is probably the result of retrofitting a dorsal fin to this P-47. Al Lloyd collection

Rear-angle view of the 56th Fighter Group's P-47s ready for a mission shows changes to D-Day invasion stripes that were phased in over several months in 1944. Around July 1944, the black-and-white D-Day identification stripes that had wrapped around fuselages and wings, top and bottom, were ordered removed from the upper surfaces. In the photo, some of the P-47s show evidence of newer, darker paint where these top-surface invasion stripes had recently been. Around September 1944 the stripes were to come off wing undersides as well, leaving only lower fuselage invasion stripes intact. USAFA/Brown

With a bubble canopy to give the pilot better visibility, a later production P-47D (44-19909) cruised over England in natural metal finish, with the identification markings of the 56th Fighter Group's 63rd Fighter Squadron displayed. Al Lloyd collection

they did not, because electrical interference made plane-to-plane communications via VHF radios almost impossible.[1] In the ensuing month, electrical bonding between the P-47s' distributors and sparkplug leads was improved as a field expedient that cleared up the interference with the radios.[2]

The combat debut for the Thunderbolts in England is often listed as April 8, 1943, when 23 Eighth Air Force fighter pilots crossed the English Channel in olive and gray P-47Cs. Squadrons of the 4th, 56th, and 78th Fighter Groups participated in a Rodeo—a fighter sweep over enemy-held territory—instead of escorting bombers.[3] Over the next week, the new Thunderbolts flew a Ramrod mission (escorting bombers over the Continent) as well as more Rodeos. On April 15, during a Rodeo over the spring-green coast of France, Major Don Blakeslee, who commanded the 4th Fighter Group's 335th Squadron, led 10 P-47s in a diving attack on a trio of Luftwaffe FW-190s. Major Blakeslee gained the first aerial victory for the P-47 that day when the Focke Wulf he fired on crashed to earth. Two other P-47 pilots each claimed an FW-190 that day; the enemy shot down one P-47, and two more Thunderbolts were lost due to engine problems.

The Eighth was beginning to feel its muscle in 1943. On May 13, 124 Thunderbolts escorted B-17s en route to a German-occupied repair depot in Meaulte, France. By early 1943, the decision had already been made to equip Eighth Air Force with P-47s solely, and to ultimately withdraw P-38 Lightnings (subsequent developments of the P-51 Mustang would later place the Mustang at the head of the hierarchy of Eighth Air Force fighters).

Thunderbolts breached German borders 30 miles deeper than ever before on July 28, 1943, surprising a force of about 60 Luftwaffe fighters and destroying 9 of them. Still, the Thunderbolts had to leave the long-ranging bombers on their own for the last leg to the target and the first leg outbound. On September 27, 1943, Eighth Air Force P-47s with belly tanks escorted B-17s all the way to their target in Germany for the first time, when the Fortresses used radar to strike the cloud-obscured port of Emden.[4] Through the winter of 1943 and into early 1944, Thunderbolts were the mainstay Eighth Air Force fighter escorts.

Evolution of escort fighter range during the war was tied to the ability to develop increased fighter fuel tankage, both external and internal. Early P-47Cs without drop

Opposite Page: When camouflage for tactical aircraft was made a local issue, variety abounded in the 56th Fighter Group. A variegated formation of P-47s shows both razorbacks and newer bubble tops in bare metal and differing interpretations of striped camouflage, as photographed from another Thunderbolt. Jerry Cole collection

Below: *Shirley* of the 353rd Fighter Group leads another razorback P-47 over England in 1943. White on the cowl and tail were, for a while, nearly universal recognition markings on olive-drab Thunderbolts in England. Jerry Cole collection

Above: Parked *Shack Rat* shows P-47 cowl flaps in the closed position for less drag and less airflow inside the cowling. The star insignia on the lower left wing was still used by some P-47s in the ETO when this photo was taken mid-1944. USAFA/Brown

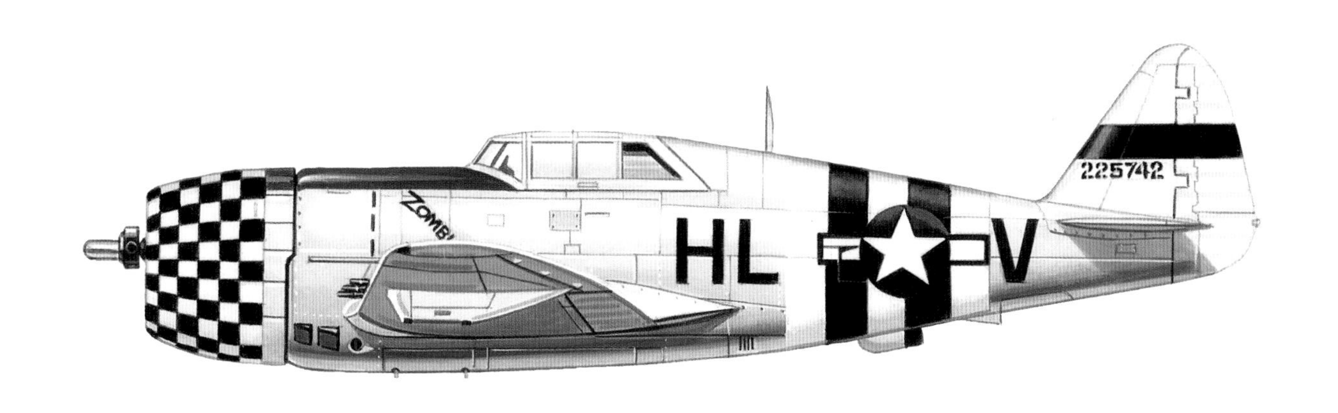

ZOMBIE, 83rd Fighter Squadron/78th Fighter Group

P-47D

tanks could only probe about 50 miles into France and the Low Countries. The introduction of 150-gallon centerline drop tanks in February 1944 gave P-47s an escort range of about 425 miles—sufficient to fly over Germany, protecting bombers at targets including Hamburg. Using a pair of underwing 108-gallon tanks that same month, Thunderbolts accompanying Eighth Air Force bombers realized an escort range of 475 miles from home, allowing penetration into Germany as deep as Frankfurt.

The heavy P-47 was known for its durability and high speed in dives. The top-scoring AAF fighter ace in Europe, Francis Gabreski, shot down 28 German aircraft from his rugged P-47D from August 24, 1943, when he prevailed over an FW-190, through July 5, 1944, when a BF-109 succumbed to Gabreski's fire near Evereux, France. A fellow Thunderbolt pilot from the same 56th Fighter Group, Robert S. Johnson, came in a close second in the ETO with 27 downed enemy aircraft. Johnson started his string in a 61st Fighter Squadron P-47C on June 13, 1943, continuing through May 8, 1944, after which he returned to the United States. The vaunted 56th Fighter Group kept its Thunderbolts as part of Eighth Air Force to the end of the war, working its way through P-47Cs, iterations of D-models, and P-47Ms before logging its final combat mission on April 21, 1945.

While some Eighth Air Force P-47s operated in natural metal finish later in the war, others remained camouflaged, some with theater-inspired variations. Early confusion between P-47s and German FW-190s led to the painting of bands on the vertical and horizontal tail surfaces, as well as a nose cowl band, on Thunderbolts. The markings were white on olive-drab aircraft and black on silver P-47s.

Though stained through the decades, this is still a compelling image of *Babe,* an early P-47D (42-74706) of the 353rd Fighter Group's 351st Fighter Squadron, probably taken late in 1943 when the aircraft was comparatively new and unscarred. Its insignia had been touched up with new blue paint to hide the short-lived red outline. By October 1944 the 353rd Group would join the exodus to P-51s in Eighth Air Force. Jerry Cole collection

They may have been classified as war weary, but these aging P-47s still had a vital service to render in Eighth Air Force. They could air-drop a dinghy to downed fliers, and help mark their location at sea for rescue. The Air Sea Rescue Squadron, variously known as Detachment B of the 65th Fighter Wing, and later as the 5th Emergency Rescue Squadron, flew from Boxted beginning in the early summer of 1944, moving to Halesworth the following January. USAFA/Brown

HAIRLESS JOE (David Schilling), 56th Fighter Group

Probably photographed between July and September 1944, this Kodachrome view of 56th Fighter Group commander David Schilling's P-47D *Hairless Joe* shows the addition of triple clusters of 4.5-inch rocket tubes under each wing for ground attack. Unorthodox green and gray camouflage is apparent in color. USAFA/Brown

Clean except for recognition markings, this P-47D (42-8001) was new with the 353rd Fighter Group when the photo was taken in the last half of 1943. This group entered combat on August 12, 1943. Jerry Cole collection

Opposite page: **A flight of early 56th Fighter Group P-47Cs and D-models in 1943 shows the presence of a yellow ring around fuselage insignia but not on wing stars.** Fred LePage collection

Above Invasion stripes under the wing date the photo post-June 6, 1944, as the 56th Fighter Group's *Belle of Belmont* carries a pair of drop tanks on the way to the runway at Boxted. A steady supply of drop tanks is stacked in the distance behind the Thunderbolt. USAFA/Brown

Below: Huge cuffed Curtiss Electric propellers adorned razorback Thunderbolts of the 78th Fighter Group, circa 1944. Gun muzzles of the nearest P-47 provided a convenient hanger for the pilot's yellow Mae West life vest. Color photographs of Eighth Air Force fields convey the fresh newness of the rapid construction that allowed so many American groups to operate from the U.K. USAFA/Brown

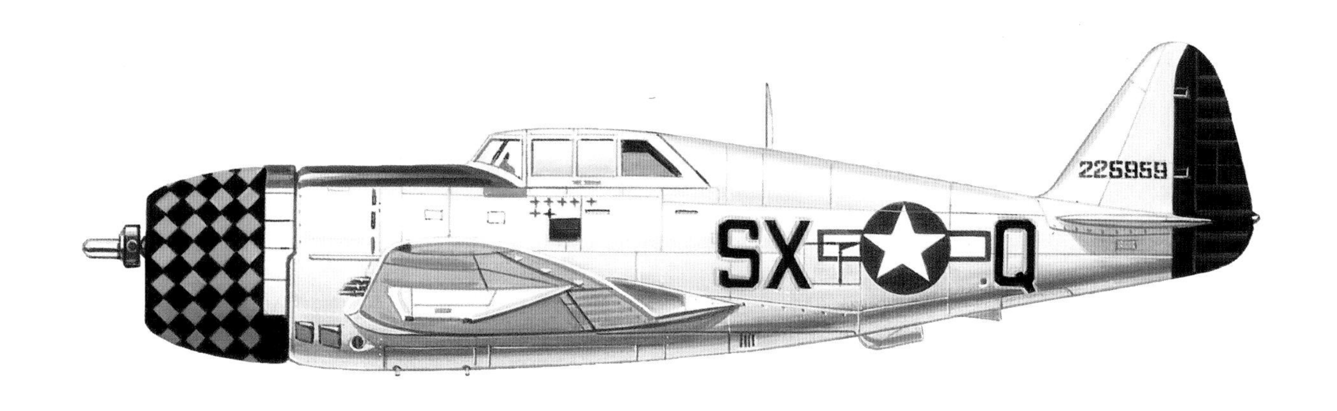
225959
SX
Q

353rd Fighter Group

LM
R
27870
16224
LM
X
LM
16347
LM
O

CHAPTER 6

P-51 Mustang

The drop tanks that helped make it possible for P-51 Mustangs to go the distance to Berlin and beyond are shackled to the wings of *Davie,* a P-51D of the 1st Scouting Force. The 1st Scouting Force was an Eighth Air Force organization that flew weather reconnaissance over targets ahead of the bomber formations. The edge around the tail is red, as is the propeller spinner and canopy frame; a white band around the nose is immediately behind the spinner. *Davie* appears to have the non-standard luxury of white sidewall mainwheel tires. Erwin Steele collection

If the Boeing B-17 has been given star status as the stereotype of the American bomber in the offensive against Germany, then the streamlined yet angular North American Aviation (NAA) P-51 Mustang is its fighter icon counterpart. Arguably, the P-51 with its high speed and, most importantly, Berlin-busting range, enabled the Eighth Air Force bomber offensive to continue and grow in 1944 and 1945.

Eager to procure warplanes from America when England was in peril in 1940, the British Purchasing Commission engaged the services of many U.S. aircraft builders. North American Aviation (NAA) was queried about the possibility of setting up an additional production line for license-built Curtiss P-40s for the British. Though the P-40 was a rugged warrior that acquitted itself well, it was also the product of pre-war thinking. North American engineers and executives proposed instead to deliver a brand-new fighter to the Royal Air Force; a fighter that embraced new thinking and new methods to vault performance ahead of the P-40. The British, perhaps already impressed with North America's trainer deliveries, and perhaps in no position to argue, went along with the NAA notion of a new fighter.

***Typhoon McGoon,* a razorback P-51B Mustang, was part of the 357th Fighter Group's 363rd Fighter Squadron. As with P-47s, Mustangs flying out of England used stripes and nose paint as recognition features. Merlin-engined razorback Mustangs were good; the ultimate visibility provided by the bubble-top P-51D improved the breed even more.** Fred LePage collection

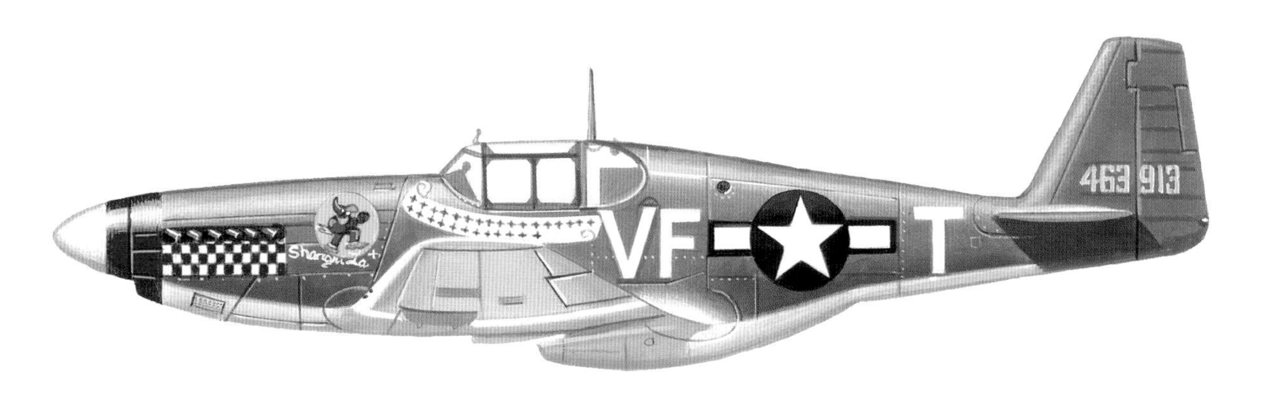

SHANGRI LA [Don Gentile]

P-51B

Pilot Lieutenant D. A. Sass held on to the externally mounted rearview mirror on his 20th Fighter Group P-51. Gun muzzles have been taped shut to keep foreign matter out; the first time they would be fired, the blast would easily blow the tape away. AFHRA

Using computations to guide their efforts to a greater extent than with previous designs, the North American team created a slim, smooth, angular prototype that crammed everything under a flush-riveted skin that seemed to employ constriction to minimize drag. NAA engineers Carter Hartley and Roy Liming worked mathematical analyses enabling them to derive the best contour between two points on the airframe. The resulting prototype did not look like most other fighters of the day. Gone were the almost art deco curves of the P-38, P-39, and P-40. With squared wingtips and tail and a fuselage that just cleared its engine and cockpit opening, the prototype resembled a speed racer. The prototype, called NA-73 by the company, first flew on October 26, 1940. The first production model for the British, named Mustang I, made its maiden flight on May 1, 1941.

From this initial batch of British Mustangs, two were diverted to the AAF as XP-51s. Performance of this first fighter, powered with an Allison V-1710-39 engine, topped out at 382 miles per hour at 13,000 feet. Though already superior in speed to any production P-40 variants, the Mustang was not yet a war-winner.[1]

Production continued, with razorback Mustangs serving with the Royal Air Force and contemporary P-51As entering AAF service. An offshoot, the Allison-powered A-36 dive bomber, incorporated speed brakes in its wings. While the P-51A inched its performance envelope up and out with a top speed of 390 miles per hour at 20,000 feet, Allison's mechanical supercharging had not yet evolved sufficiently to deliver competitive performance at high altitude. The P-51B would change all that. In 1942, a proposal from the U.S. military attaché in London urged blending the competitive P-51 airframe with the superb Rolls Royce Merlin engine to gain a performance advantage at altitude. Though not turbo-supercharged, the Rolls Merlin enjoyed benefits from superior mechanical supercharging. The resulting hybrids, called Mustang X by the British, furnished data

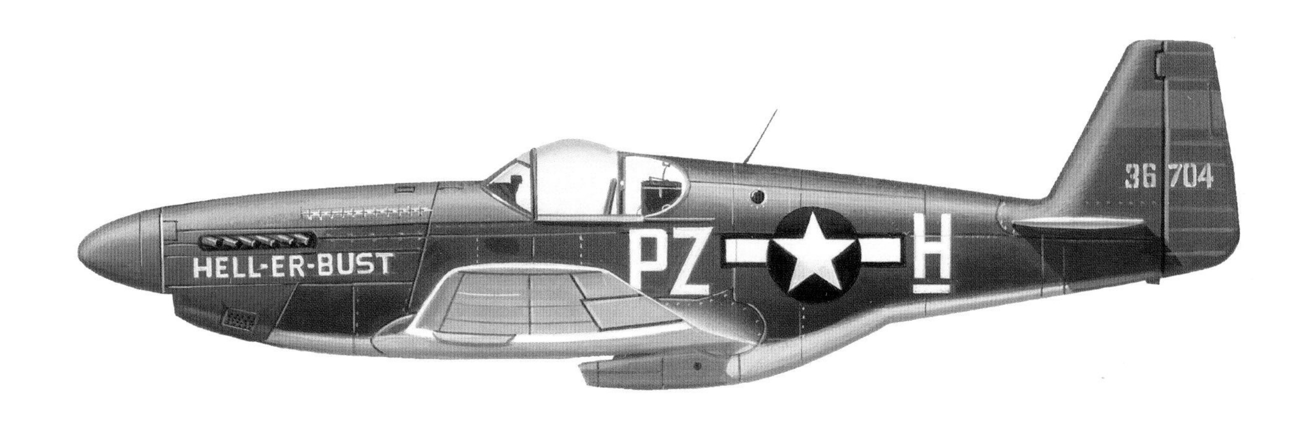

HELL-ER-BUST (Ed Heller), 486th Fighter Squadron/352 Fighter Group

The 78th Fighter Group continued its use of black-and-white checkers on the noses of its P-51s after converting from P-47s. The gray, toned down national star is readily evident against the bright silver metal of this P-51. Fred LePage collection

that enabled NAA to design a production variant that was initially called the XP-78 and later changed to the XP-51B.

The B-model Mustang represented more than a swap of powerplants. Extensive tests, including full-scale wind tunnel tests by the National Advisory Committee for Aeronautics (NACA), further refined the airframe and evolved the P-51's signature belly scoop into a rakish inlet that stood off from the fuselage surface in an effort to ingest clear air outside the turbulent boundary layer surrounding the airframe. The results were phenomenal: the Merlin-powered XP-51B, initially flown the last day of November 1942, posted a top speed of 441 miles per hour at 29,800 feet and had a service ceiling of 42,000 feet. Its license-built Packard Merlin V-1650-3 engine used a two-stage supercharger and had water injection for emergency power bursts.

Production P-51Bs, with four .50-caliber machine guns in their wings, began appearing in May 1943. Three months later, NAA's Dallas, Texas, plant began delivering the first of 1,750 similar P-51Cs. Production Bs and Cs had top speeds listed around 440 miles per hour at bomber altitudes. These razorback speedsters could carry a pair of underwing drop tanks. So equipped, range was good, but more could be done. Additional fuselage tankage behind the pilot was put aboard P-51Bs and Cs, increasing internal fuel capacity from 184 to 269 gallons. When combined with a pair of underwing drop tanks, the P-51 could now take the bombers all the way to Berlin and back, which they did beginning in March 1944. It was a rapid evolution; in January 1944, escort P-51s could range 475 miles from home, comparable to the maximum their P-47 counterparts would achieve the following month in Eighth Air Force service. By March of that year, Mustangs handily outdistanced Thunderbolts and Lightnings by successively attaining ranges of 650 and then 850 miles across Europe.

If the AAF was ignorant of the need for hard-hitting long-range escort fighters as the bomber offensive began,

It was a beautiful day for flying above patchy clouds when *TIKA-IV* of the 361st Fighter Group was photographed in color. Exhaust constituents have deposited a visible layer over part of the fuselage national insignia. The pilot grinned from his perch near six victory marks painted just below the canopy. AAF

Tail number 43-7139 identifies this 352nd Fighter Group Mustang over France as a P-51B. It was the teaming of long-range escort fighters like the P-51 with the B-17 and B-24 that enabled Eighth Air Force to keep pressure on Germany. The fighters did not simply escort the bombers; sometimes they ranged ahead and engaged the Luftwaffe in a war of attrition in an effort to neutralize German defensive fighter strength. If Eighth Air Force bombers did not enjoy air supremacy by war's end, they at least had their passage made much safer by the aggressive actions of friendly fighters.
AAF via 446th Bomb Group

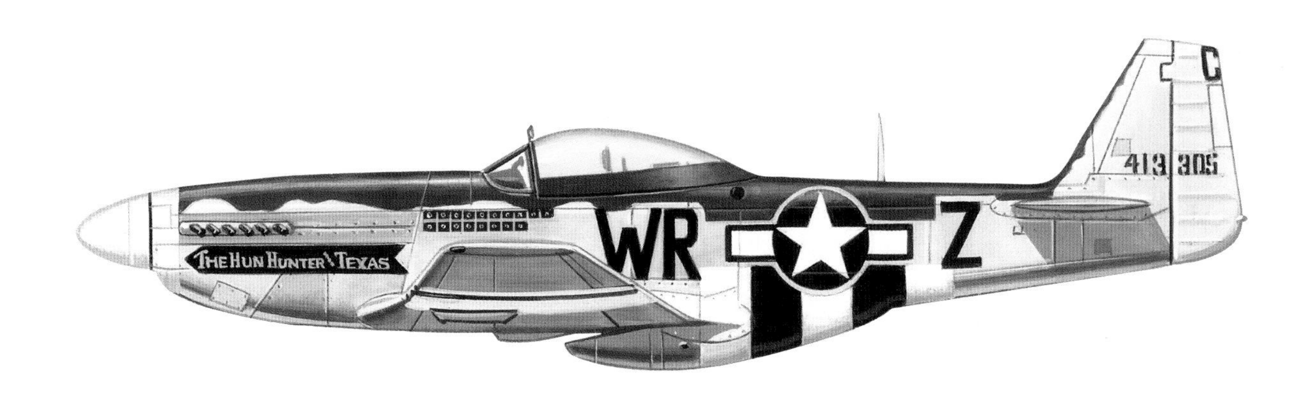

THE HUN HUNTER FROM TEXAS [Henry Brown], 354th Fighter Squadron/355th Fighter Group

P-51D

their redemption in the form of the Merlin-powered Mustang was a remarkable turnaround. Though no fighter could guarantee total bomber safety, the lack of escorts for deep penetrations over Germany altogether could have gravely delayed, and perhaps even thwarted, Eighth Air Force's strategic bombardment campaign.

The signature P-51D, which introduced a large bubble canopy for greater all-around pilot visibility, followed the successful P-51B and similar Texas-built P-51C. The D-model also increased the number of machine guns buried in the wings to six (which had been done to some, but not all, earlier Bs and Cs). The P-51D hit 437 miles per hour at 25,000 feet. Eighth Air Force readily embraced P-51Bs, Cs, and Ds. Even as other model letters were assigned to experimental Mustang variants that did not see World War II combat, another production version, the P-51K, did enter service. It was essentially a P-51D fitted with an Aeroproducts propeller instead of the D-model's Hamilton-Standard prop.

Even the war-winning P-51D was not without quirks. To stow sufficient fuel for deep penetration missions, a less-than-ideal, aft center of gravity condition could prevail in the early part of the flight until fuel was burned off and better balance was achieved. A British report bluntly noted, "The ditching performance of the Mustang is so bad that pilots should bale out on every occasion if sufficient height exists to do this." The racy underslung coolant scoop acted as an abrupt brake upon contacting the water, and could plow a P-51 under the waves.[2]

On November 12, 1944, Eighth Air Force established 270 hours as the measure of an operational tour of duty for its fighter pilots.[3] By that time, the vast majority of them were logging it in Mustangs.

This white-ruddered, red-nosed P-51D-NA (44-14137) flew with Eighth Air Force's 4th Fighter Group when photographed in 1945. Two pilots are crammed in the cockpit in this photo as they reenact a daring rescue in Germany when one of the pilots landed on an open field to rescue another who had just been shot down. AAF via AFHRA

BETTY LEE III (William Kemp), 375th Fighter Squadron/361st Fighter Group

In a reenactment back at their English base, 4th Fighter Group pilots Lieutenant George D. Green (with flying helmet) and Major Pierce W. McKennon demonstrate how they shared one oxygen mask when Green rescued McKennon from a field 40 miles north of Berlin on March 18, 1945. Green landed near McKennon, who had bailed out of his Mustang moments before. Germans with a leashed dog approached, as other P-51s harassed them while McKennon and Green figured out how they could both occupy the single-seat Mustang and make a clean getaway. AFHRA

Janey Girl From Texas **has the brightly unmistakable black-and-white bars of the 20th Fighter Group on the sides of the nose on this bubble-top P-51 Mustang. Captain W. R. Yarbrough flew the Mustang.** AFHRA

Pilots of the 4th Fighter Group climbed on the P-51D ***Ridge Runner*** **for this 1945 portrait. Nose and spinner are red. Fourteen victory crosses told of this aircraft's exploits.** AAF photo

MAN O'WAR [Clairborne Kinnard], 355th Fighter Group

Bluenosed 352nd Fighter Group razorback P-51 *Lilli Marlene* banks away from a 446th Bomb Group B-24 over France in September 1944. By the time of this photo, black-and-white invasion stripes had been removed from the wing undersurfaces, as evidenced by color variations. AAF via 446th Bomb Group

Painted Pony

P-51Bs and Cs reached England in olive and gray camouflage. Later, some of these razorback Mustangs flew over Europe in natural metal finish. Normal coloring for P-51Ds was natural metal. In Eighth service, some later P-51s reverted to camouflage upper surfaces, often retaining bare metal undersurfaces, as their pilots sought to mask their fighters from German fighter pilots looking down from higher altitudes. The requirement to wrap the inboard wing area and aft fuselage in alternating black and white stripes as quick identification markings for the Normandy invasion was subsequently modified by removing the stripes from upper surfaces as the Allies' foothold on the Continent solidified. This led to some artistic variations on 361st Fighter Group Mustangs, as dark blue paint was sometimes used to cover the upper surface stripes on wings and fuselage.

Early identity confusion between razorback P-51s and BF-109s led to the adoption of white stripes on Mustang tails, noses, and even wings as quick identification tools. Once entered into the Eighth Air Force inventory, P-51s remained and grew in number as P-38s and P-47s were replaced.

Details of Lieutenant George D. Green's 4th Fighter Group P-51D (44-14137) include the label by the cockpit naming his crew chief, assistant crew chief, and armorer; and the red canopy frame. Green's Mustang flew from Berlin to England with two men in one seat. AFHRA

The war was over when local residents visited the home of the 78th Fighter Group at Duxford and inspected P-51D *Contrary Mary* on August 1, 1945. The Mustang's canopy frame carried its victory tallies. AAF

A mixed bunch of Mustangs, some razorback, some bubble top with and without dorsal fins, represented the 361st Fighter Group for a color portrait taken in the last half of 1944. Dark paint has been used to partially camouflage the P-51s while deleting the invasion stripes from their upper fuselage surfaces, which was called for by July 1944. AAF/NARA

CHAPTER 7

Miscellaneous Eighth Air Force Aircraft

The Army Air Forces' desire to prune the logistics tree and emphasize only a few key aircraft types for Eighth Air Force use was a logical and prudent effort based on efficiency. Yet, from 1942 to 1945, a gaggle of miscellaneous aircraft types served the Eighth for a variety of reasons. Availability of British utility types aided the Eighth's need for transports to connect its vast network of bases in the English countryside. And, especially early in the war when the Eighth's efforts at building its force was impeded by the diversion of aircraft to North Africa, it behooved the Eighth to take what it could get. Given the nature of some wartime appropriations of individual airplanes by units under the Eighth Air Force, it may be impossible to tally all of the types that served the Eighth, officially or unofficially. Among those less common aircraft rendering service to the Eighth were the following.

The 4th Fighter Group operated Supermarine Spitfires for a while before converting to P-47s in March 1943 and later switching to Mustangs. This example belonged to the 335th Fighter Squadron, and was still around when the red-bordered national insignia was introduced in the summer of 1943. NARA

A 388th Bomb Group photographer photographed a British Airspeed Oxford twin-engine transport as the aircraft acquired an appropriate nickname, *Len'leas,* on October 27, 1943. USAFA/Brown

A Martin B-26B quickly passes the camera during the first Eighth Air Force Marauder mission on May 14, 1943. AAF/AFHRA

Salutes are rendered as Eighth Air Force B-26 Marauders make their combat debut on May 14, 1943. Eighth Air Force forays into medium and light bombing did not have the impact of the daylight heavy precision bombardment effort. AAF

Whirling propellers mark the passage of an Eighth Air Force Martin B-26 Marauder on the Eighth's first Marauder mission on May 14, 1943. AAF/AFHRA

It was congratulations all around in February 1945 as the 7th Photo Group of the Eighth Air Force logged the 4000th sortie, in a silver-painted Spitfire IX. The pilot was Lieutenant J. H. Roberts of the 14th Photo Reconnaissance Squadron. AAF/AFHRA

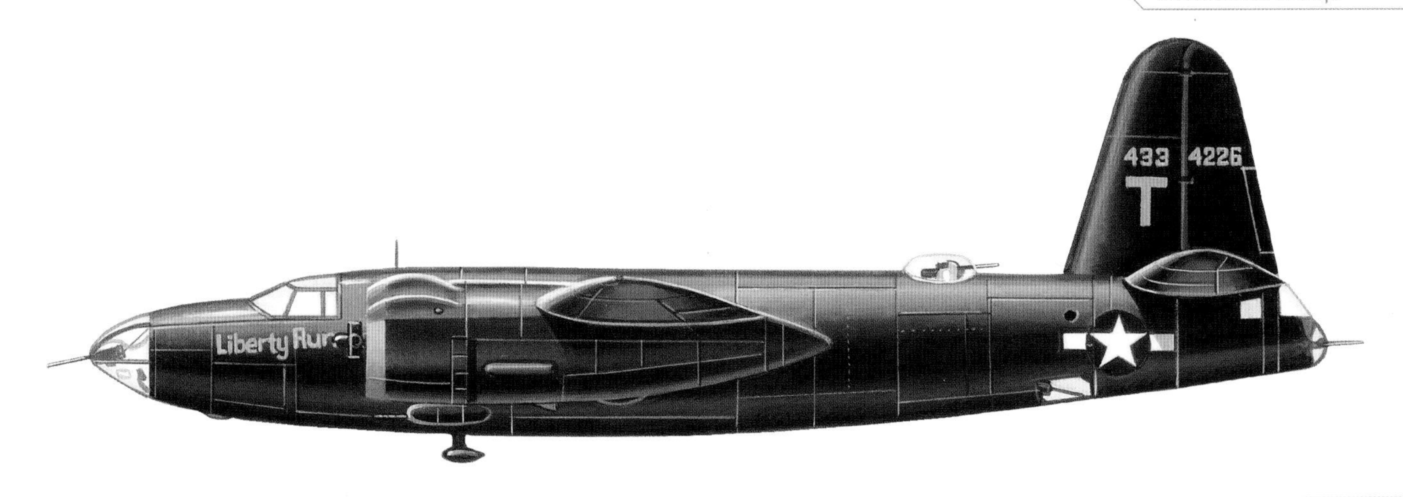

LIBERTY RUN, 654th Bomb Group

Martin B-26 Marauder

The Martin B-26 Marauder was a twin-engine bomber powered by R2800 radial engines. The B-26Bs and B-26Cs used briefly by Eighth Air Force could carry about 3,000 pounds of bombs. They had a range of around 1,150 miles. Cruising speed could vary from about 260 miles per hour in some early B-models to about 214 miles per hour in B-26Cs and late B-models, according to published statistics. They carried as many as a dozen .50-caliber machine guns in fixed, flexible, and turret mounts. During B-model production, the wingspan was increased from 65 feet to 71 feet; fuselage length was 58 feet, 3 inches. A larger vertical fin introduced with the wing change also increased height from 19 feet, 10 inches, to 21 feet, 6 inches. From B-models through C-models, gross weight varied from 34,000 pounds to 38,200 pounds.

Eighth Air Force brought the B-26 to England in February 1943. First combat use of Marauders by the Eighth came on May 14, 1943, when the 322nd Bomb Group sent 11 B-26s as part of a strike package that included 198 four-engine heavy bombers. The grand total of 209 bombers gave the young Eighth Air Force its first 200-plus bomber mission day. The B-26s attacked a power station in Ijmuiden, Holland, that day and skimmed trees at 50 feet on the way in, popping up to 100 feet to drop their bombs. Only three days later, another low-level B-26 mission saw 10 Marauders reach the Continent; all were destroyed, prompting a cessation of Eighth Air Force B-26 sorties while the harsh lessons of combat were sorted out.

The Eighth's B-26s did not resume combat until July 16, 1943, when 14 Marauders went after railyards at Abbeville. As the summer of 1943 grew old, the Eighth's few B-26s made strikes in France. Near the end of their service in the Eighth Air Force, on October 3, 1943, nearly 200 Marauder sorties were logged against German-held airfields at four sites on the Continent. In the Eighth's combat choreography, B-26 airfield strikes were timed to deny the Germans use of those fields and their fighters against heavy bomber formations. Ultimately, Eighth Air Force B-26s flew with the 322nd, 323rd, 386th, and 387th Bomb Groups. But their tenure as part of the mighty Eighth Air Force was limited. By October 16, a scant five months after entering the war from their bases in England, all Marauders assigned to Eighth Air Force were transferred to the tactical Ninth Air Force.[1]

The B-26B and C-models operated by the Eighth in 1943 were camouflaged with olive upper surfaces and gray lower surfaces. Squadron and individual aircraft code letters appeared in dark gray on the aft fuselages of the B-26s. Initially, Eighth Air Force Marauders entered combat with the 1942-style blue disk national insignia lacking white bars; later application of white bars sometimes partially obscured identification letters.

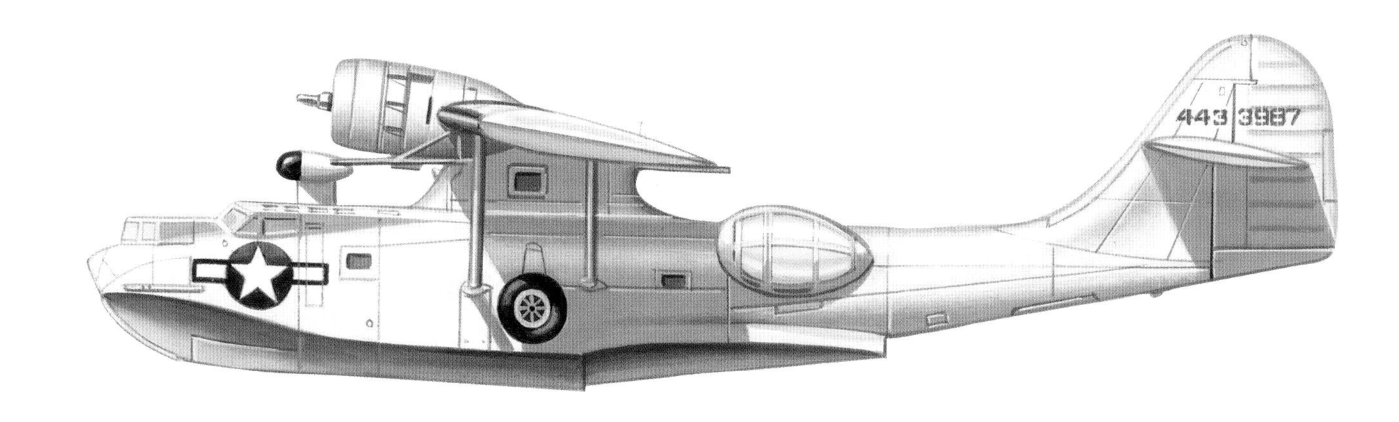

OA-10A CATALINA

Consolidated OA-10A Catalina

Consolidated Aircraft's venerable old naval PBY Catalina flying-boat design served the Eighth Air Force as the AAF's amphibious OA-10A variant of the PBY-5A. From January to May 1945, the Eighth's 5th Emergency Rescue Squadron (ERS) flew about 12 all-white OA-10As with dark serial numbers, and an absence of other unit markings. Two of Eighth Air Force's small fleet of OA-10As were ultimately listed as missing in action. Army Air Force OA-10As were built by Vickers in Canada.

The OA-10A had a wingspan of 104 feet; a length of 63 feet, 10 inches; a height of 20 feet, 2 inches; and a gross weight of 35,420 pounds. Its two Pratt and Whitney R1830-92 engines gave the Catalina a top speed of 175 miles an hour at 7,000 feet, and a leisurely cruising speed of 113 miles an hour. Its range was 2,350 miles.

Search & Rescue P-47 and B-17

The Eighth Air Force employed war-weary P-47 Thunderbolt fighters for air sea rescue as a detachment of the 65th Fighter Wing in early May 1944, later becoming the Fifth ERS (see above). The Thunderbolts carried air-droppable dinghies and smoke markers to aid in the rescue of downed fliers in the waters bounding England.

In the last few months of combat in 1945, the 5th ERS operated a B-17G fitted with a large lifeboat beneath the bomb bay for dropping to downed aircrews. In the final tally, the P-47s logged more than 3,450 sorties; the OA-10As accounted for more than 115 sorties, and the B-17 had 16 sorties.

Spitfire

A striped search and rescue P-47 shared parking space with a turretless B-17F-DL (42-3089) bearing the Square-C markings of the 96th Bomb Group, circa mid-1944. USAFA/Brown

A Spitfire Vb of the 31st Fighter Group, 309th Fighter Squadron, remained in England after the group departed Eighth Air Force. The 31st operated Spitfires as part of the Eighth Air Force in 1942. AAF/NARA

The Eighth Air Force first acquired British Supermarine Spitfire Vb fighters in 1942 to equip fighter units including the 4th, 31st, and 52nd Fighter Groups. But only the 4th would remain in Eighth Air Force for the duration. Worthy as the Spitfire was, the machines used by the 4th Fighter Group in 1942 and early 1943 naturally gave way to a succession of P-47 Thunderbolts and evolved long-range P-51 Mustangs as the ultimate escort fighters. The Spitfire fighters of the early Eighth Air Force retained typical RAF day fighter camouflage colors consisting of Dark Green and Ocean Gray upper surfaces with Medium Sea Gray undersurfaces.

Photo reconnaissance Spitfires remained on strength with the Eighth Air Force's 7th Photo Group into 1945. Colors were Photo Reconnaissance Blue and sometimes included aluminum-silver paint.

Several Troop Carrier groups had brief stays in England as part of the Eighth Air Force before moving on to North Africa around November 1942 to help anchor the Twelfth Air Force. Troop Carrier Douglas C-47s and similar (small door) C-53s carried few markings beyond standard olive camouflage broken with green blotching, and possibly a letter on the aft fuselage, during that era. This can be seen in two snapshots of ex-Eighth Air Force C-47s/C-53s from the 62nd Troop Carrier Group soon after it joined Twelfth Air Force in North Africa. The terrain in the flight view is the Atlas Mountains. Raleigh Smith photos

UC-64 NORSEMAN

C-47 and C-53

Douglas C-47 and C-53 transports were carried on the roster of the Eighth Air Force in strength briefly in 1942. The buildup of aircraft for Eighth Air Force objectives in 1942 saw several Troop Carrier Groups—the 60th, 62nd, 64th, and 315th—migrate to England. With the exception of the 315th, these units were quickly reassigned to Twelfth Air Force later that year. The 315th sent a detachment to Algeria in May 1943, and the entire unit was reassigned to Ninth Air Force that October.

The C-53 was essentially the small-door military equivalent of the successful DC-3 airliner; the C-47 employed a larger double cargo door on the left side of the fuselage to enable bulky items to be carried, or paratroops to be airdropped. These Douglas twins had wingspans of 95 feet, 6 inches, and fuselage lengths of 63 feet, 9 inches. Height was 17 feet. Pratt and Whitney R1830 engines gave the planes a typical cruising speed of about 135 miles per hour and a range of 1,600 miles.

Miscellaneous

Aircraft known to have served Eighth Air Force in at least minor roles include the North American AT-6 Texan single-engine trainer, Noorduyn UC-64 Norseman single-engine fabric-covered cabin monoplane, Piper L-4B Grasshopper, Airspeed Oxford, Douglas A-26B Invader, deHavilland Mosquito, Douglas Boston III, Douglas A-20B, Vultee A-35 Vengeance, and Martin AT-23 target-towing and training variant of the B-26 Marauder.

Eighth Air Force units obtained a wide variety of aircraft for miscellaneous duties. The 446th Bomb Group had a silver Noorduyn C-64 Norseman (44-70260), complete with the group's yellow and black tail colors. A 600-horsepower R-1340 engine powered the Canadian-built Norseman. AFHRA

CHAPTER 1

1. *Army Air Forces Statistical Digest, World War II,* Office of Statistical Control, HQ, USAAF, December 1945.
2. Maurer Maurer, *Air Force Combat Units of World War II,* Office of Air Force History, Washington, D.C., 1983.
3. Ibid.
4. Ibid.
5. Ibid.
6. Maurer Maurer, *World War II Combat Squadrons of the United States Air Force,* Smithmark Publishers, New York, N.Y., 1992.
7. Kit C. Carter and Robert Mueller, compilers, *Combat Chronology 1941–1945—U.S. Army Air Forces in World War II,* Center for Air Force History, Washington, D.C., 1991.
8. Ibid.
9. *Target: Germany—The Army Air Forces' Official Story of the VIII Bomber Command's First Year over Europe,* Simon and Schuster, New York, N.Y., 1943.
10. Hugh Odishaw, "Radar Bombing in the 8th Air Force," under the supervision of the Radiation Laboratory Historical Office, 1946.
11. Carter and Mueller, compilers, *Combat Chronology 1941–1945.*

CHAPTER 2

1. Peter M. Bowers, *Fortress in the Sky,* Sentry Books, Granada Hills, Calif., 1976.
2. Frederick A. Johnsen, *B-17 Flying Fortress—The Symbol of Second World War Air Power,* McGraw-Hill, New York, N.Y., 2000.
3. Frederick A. Johnsen, *Boeing B-17 Flying Fortress,* Warbird Tech Series, Vol. 7, Specialty Press, North Branch, Minn., 2001.
4. *History of the Army Air Forces Proving Ground Command, Part 12: Testing of the B-17 and B-24,* Historical Branch, Army Air Forces Proving Ground Command, Eglin Field, Fla., 1945.
5. Ibid.
6. Memo, subject: "Report on YB-40 Aircraft," from Colonel William M. Reid, Commander, 92nd Bomb Group, to Commanding General, VIII Bomber Command, 7 July 1943, AFHRA.
7. Roger A. Freeman, *The Mighty Eighth – A History of the U.S. 8th Army Air Force,* Doubleday, Garden City, N.Y. 1970.
8. "Operational Results with Disney," *Air Intelligence Digest* No. 1, HQ, Army Air Forces Center, Directorate of Operations and Training, Combat Intelligence Branch, Orlando, Fl., 1 July 1945.
9. Dana Bell, *Air Force Colors, Vol. 2—ETO & MTO—1942–45,* Squadron/Signal Publications, Carrollton, Tex., 1980.

CHAPTER 3

1. *Army Air Forces Statistical Digest, World War II,* Office of Statistical Control, HQ, USAAF, December 1945.
2. Letter, Lieutenant General J. H. Doolittle, USA, Commanding, HQ Eighth Air Force, to Lieutenant General Barney M. Giles, Chief of Air Staff, HQ Army Air Forces, 25 Jan., 1945 on file at AFHRA.
3. Ibid.
4. Freeman, *The Mighty Eighth.*
5. Letter, Lieutenant General J. H. Doolittle, USA, Commanding, HQ Eighth Air Force, to Lieutenant General Barney M. Giles, Chief of Air Staff, HQ Army Air Forces, 25 Jan., 1945, on file at AFHRA.
6. Bowers, *Fortress in the Sky;* and Frederick A. Johnsen, *B-24 Liberator – Rugged But Right,* McGraw-Hill, New York, N.Y. 1999.
7. Technical Report, Air Technical Section (Eighth AF), Subject: "Operational Aircraft Losses in Connection with the Use of Hamilton Standard 'Hydromatic' propellers," 27 Jan., 1945.
8. Ibid.
9. Frederick A. Johnsen, *Consolidated B-24 Liberator,* Vol. 1, Warbird Tech Series, Specialty Press, North Branch, Minn., 2001.
10. Allan G. Blue, *The B-24 Liberator,* Charles Scribner's Sons, New York, N.Y., 1975.
11. Carter and Mueller, compilers, *Combat Chronology 1941–1945.*

CHAPTER 4

1. Benjamin S. Kelsey, *The Dragon's Teeth? The Creation of United States Air Power for World War II,* Smithsonian Institution Press, Washington, D.C., 1982.
2. Ibid.
3. Freeman, *The Mighty Eighth.*
4. Ibid.
5. Richard G. Davis, *Carl A. Spaatz and the Air War in Europe,* Center for Air Force History, Washington, D.C., 1993.
6. Frederick A. Johnsen, *Lockheed P-38 Lightning,* Warbird Tech Series, Vol. 2, Specialty Press, North Branch, Minn., 1996.
7. Ibid.
8. Carter and Mueller, compilers, *Combat Chronology 1941–1945*; Freeman, *The Mighty Eighth.*

CHAPTER 5

1. Carter and Mueller, compilers, *Combat Chronology 1941–1945.*
2. Freeman, *The Mighty Eighth.*
3. Kenn C. Rust, *Eighth Air Force Story,* Historical Aviation Album, Temple City, Calif., 1978.
4. Carter and Mueller, compilers, *Combat Chronology 1941–1945.*

CHAPTER 6

1. Ray Wagner, *American Combat Planes,* Doubleday, Garden City, 1968.
2. Frederick A. Johnsen, *North American P-51 Mustang,* Warbird Tech Series, Vol. 5, Specialty Press, North Branch, Minn., 1996.
3. Carter and Mueller, compilers, *Combat Chronology 1941–1945.*

CHAPTER 7

1. Frederick A. Johnsen, *Martin B-26 Marauder,* Warbird Tech Series Vol. 29, Specialty Press, North Branch, Minn., 2000.

Major Eighth Air Force Units

GROUP	SQUADRONS	AIRCRAFT	DATES
25th Bomb Group	652nd, 653rd, 654th	B-24, B-17, Mosquito, B-25, B-26, P-38, L-5	'44–45
34th Bomb Group	4th, 7th, 18th, 391st	B-24, B-17	'44–45
44th Bomb Group	66th, 67th, 68th, 506th	B-24	'42–45
91st Bomb Group	322nd, 323rd, 324th, 401st	B-17	'42–45
92nd Bomb Group	325th, 326th, 327th, 407th	B-17, YB-40	'42–45
93rd Bomb Group	328th, 329th, 330th, 409th	B-24	'42–45
94th Bomb Group	331st, 332nd, 333rd, 410th	B-17	'43–45
95th Bomb Group	334th 335th, 336th, 412th	B-17	'43–45
96th Bomb Group	337th, 338th, 339th, 413th	B-17	'43–45
97th Bomb Group	340th, 341st, 342nd, 414th	B-17	'42
100th Bomb Group	349th, 350th, 351st, 418th	B-17	'43–45
301st Bomb Group	32nd, 352nd, 353rd, 419th	B-17	'42
303rd Bomb Group	358th, 359th, 360th, 427th	B-17	'42–45
305th Bomb Group	364th, 365th, 366th, 422nd	B-17	'42–45
306th Bomb Group	367th, 368th, 369th, 423rd	B-17	'42–45
322nd Bomb Group	449th, 450th, 451st, 452nd	B-26	'43
323rd Bomb Group	453rd, 454th, 455th, 456th	B-26	'43
351st Bomb Group	508th, 509th, 510th, 511th	B-17	'43–45
379th Bomb Group	524th, 525th, 526th, 527th	B-17	'43–45
381st Bomb Group	532nd, 533rd, 534th, 535th	B-17	'43–45
384th Bomb Group	544th, 545th, 546th, 547th	B-17	'43–45
385th Bomb Group	548th, 549th, 550th, 551st	B-17	'43–45
386th Bomb Group	552nd, 553rd, 554th, 555th	B-26	'43
387th Bomb Group	556th, 557th, 558th, 559th	B-26	'43
388th Bomb Group	560th, 561st, 562nd, 563rd	B-17	'43–45
389th Bomb Group	564th, 565th, 566th, 567th	B-24	'43–45
390th Bomb Group	568th, 569th, 570th, 571st	B-17	'43–45
392nd Bomb Group	576th, 577th, 578th, 579th	B-24	'43–45

GROUP	SQUADRONS	AIRCRAFT	DATES
398th Bomb Group	600th, 601st, 602nd, 603rd	B-17	'44–45
401st Bomb Group	612th, 613th, 614th, 615th	B-17	'43–45
445th Bomb Group	700th, 701st, 702nd, 703rd	B-24	'43–45
446th Bomb Group	704th, 705th, 706th, 707th	B-24	'43–45
447th Bomb Group	708th, 709th, 710th, 711th	B-17	'43–45
448th Bomb Group	712th, 713th, 714th, 715th	B-24	'43–45
452nd Bomb Group	728th, 729th, 730th, 731st	B-17	'44–45
453rd Bomb Group	732nd, 733rd, 734th, 735th	B-24	'44–45
457th Bomb Group	748th, 749th, 750th, 751st	B-17	'44–45
458th Bomb Group	752nd, 753rd, 754th, 755th	B-24	'44–45
466th Bomb Group	784th, 785th, 786th, 787th	B-24	'44–45
467th Bomb Group	788th, 789th, 790th, 791st	B-24	'44–45
482nd Bomb Group	812th, 813th, 814th	B-24, B-17	'43–45
486th Bomb Group	832nd, 833rd, 834th, 835th	B-24, B-17	'44–45
487th Bomb Group	836th, 837th, 838th, 839th	B-24, B-17	'44–45
489th Bomb Group	844th, 845th, 846th, 847th	B-24	'44
490th Bomb Group	848th, 849th, 850th, 851st	B-24, B-17	'44–45
491st Bomb Group	852nd, 853rd, 854th, 855th	B-24	'44–45
492nd Bomb Group	856th, 857th, 858th, 859th	B-24	'44–45
493rd Bomb Group	860th, 861st, 862nd, 863rd	B-24, B-17	'44–45
1st Fighter Group	27th, 71st, 94th	P-38	'42
4th Fighter Group	334th, 335th, 336th	Spitfire, P-47, P-51	'42–45
14th Fighter Group	48th, 49th, 50th	P-38	'42
20th Fighter Group	55th, 77th, 79th	P-38, P-51	'43–45
31st Fighter Group	307th, 308th, 309th	Spitfire	'42
52nd Fighter Group	2nd, 4th, 5th	Spitfire	'42
55th Fighter Group	38th, 338th, 343rd	P-38, P-51	'43–45
56th Fighter Group	61st, 62nd, 63rd	P-47	'43–45
78th Fighter Group	82nd, 83rd, 84th	P-38, P-47, P-51	'43–45
82nd Fighter Group	95th, 96th, 97th	P-38	'42
339th Fighter Group	503rd, 504th, 505th	P-51	'44–45
350th Fighter Group	345th, 346th, 347th	P-400, Spitfire	'42
352nd Fighter Group	328th, 486th, 487th	P-47, P-51	'43–45
353rd Fighter Group	350th, 351st, 352nd	P-47, P-51	'43–45
355th Fighter Group	354th, 357th, 358th	P-47, P-51	'43–45
356th Fighter Group	359th, 360th, 361st	P-47, P-51	'43–45
357th Fighter Group	362nd, 363rd, 364th	P-51	'44–45
358th Fighter Group	365th, 366th, 367th	P-47	'43–44
359th Fighter Group	368th, 369th, 370th	P-47, P-51	'43–45
361st Fighter Group	374th, 375th, 376th	P-47, P-51	'43–45
364th Fighter Group	383rd, 384th, 385th	P-38, P-51	'44–45

REFERENCES:

Maurer Maurer, editor, *Air Force Combat Units of World War II*, Office of Air Force History, 1983; Kenn C. Rust, *Eighth Air Force Story, Historical Aviation Album*, 1978; Roger A. Freeman, *The Mighty Eighth: A History of the U.S. 8th Army Air Force*, Doubleday, 1970; Rene J. Francillon, *USAAF Fighter Units—*Europe 1942–45, Sky Books Press, 1977.

Units listed only for 1942 typically were quickly reassigned to Twelfth Air Force as the AAF built up its European and Middle Eastern forces simultaneously, albeit with limited resources. Ranking Eighth Air Force officers complained that the diversion of assets away from England was detrimental to the Eighth's timetable for strategic bombardment of German targets. With the exception of some of the early units organized in 1942 that were soon moved to Twelfth Air Force, the dates shown are the years in which the units flew combat for Eighth Air Force.

The listing for the 492nd Bomb Group tells only part of that unit's unique story. Known as the Carpetbaggers, this unit airdropped secret agents and important supplies behind enemy lines.

GROUP		SQUADRONS	AIRCRAFT	DATES
495th	Fighter Training Gp	551st, 552nd	P-47	'43–45
496th	Fighter Training Gp	554th, 555th	P-38, P-51	'43–45
479th	Fighter Group	434th, 435th, 436th	P-38, P-51	'44–45
60th	Troop Carrier Group	10th, 11th, 12th, 28th	C-47	'42
62nd	Troop Carrier Group	4th, 7th, 8th, 51st	C-47, C-53	'42
64th	Troop Carrier Group	16th, 17th, 18th, 35th, 54th	C-47	'42
315th	Troop Carrier Group	33rd, 34th, 35th, 43rd, 54th	C-47	'42–43
3rd	Photo Group	5th, 12th, 13th, 14th, 15th	F-4, F-5, B-17	'42
7th	Photo Group	13th, 14th, 22nd, 27th P-51D, Spitfire	F-4, F-5, F-6,	'43–45
67th	Recon Group	12th, 107th, 109th, 153rd	Spitfire, L-4, A-20	'42–43
5t	Emergency Rescue Squadron		P-47, OA-10A, B-17	'44–45
15th	Bombardment Sqdn		Boston (DB-7)	'42

Royal Air Force Spitfires escorted Eighth Air Force heavy bombers on occasion, but were limited in range. The pilot of this clipped-wing variant is wearing large British headphones also adopted by some American fighter pilots. Fred LePage collection

Representative Eighth Air Force and Luftwaffe Aircraft Specifications

This artistic image captures contrails as spirals corkscrewing behind B-17Gs of the 452nd Bomb Group. USAFA/Brown

TYPE	SPEEDS	RANGE	CEILING	BOMB LOAD	WEIGHTS (EMPTY/GROSS)	LENGTH/SPAN
EIGHTH AF						
B-17E	195–223/317 mph	2,000 mi.	36,600 ft	4,000 lb	32,250/40,260 lb w/4,000 lb. of bombs	73'10'/103'9"
B-17F	200/299 mph	1,300 mi.	37,500 ft	6,000 lb	34,000/55,000 lb w/6000 lb. of bombs	74'9"/103'9"
B-17G	182/287 mph	2,000 mi.	35,600 ft	6,000 lb	36,135/55,000 lb w/6,000 lb. of bombs	74'4"/103'9"
B-24D	200/303 mph	2,850 mi.	32,000 ft	6,000 lb	32,605/55,000 lb w/5,000 lb. of bombs	66'4"/110'
B-24J	215/290 mph	2,100 mi.	28,000 ft	6,000 lb	36,500/56,000 lb w/5,000 lb. of bombs	67'2"/110'
P-38F	305/395 mph	1,925 mi.	39,000 ft		12,264/15,900 lb maximum	37'10"/52'
P-38J	290/414 mph	2,600 mi.	44,000 ft	3,200 lb	12,780/17,500 lb maximum	37'10"/52'
P-47C	350/433 mph	1,250 mi.	42,000 ft		9,900/13,500 lb maximum	36'1"/40'9"
P-47D-25	350/428 mph	1,700 mi.	42,000 ft		10,000/14,500 lb maximum	36'1"/40'9"
P-47M	/473 mph	530 mi.	41,000 ft		10,423/13,275 lb normal	36'4"/40'9"
P-51B	244–343/440 mph	2,200 mi.	42,000 ft		6,985/9,800 lb maximum	32'3"/37'
P-51D	362/437 mph	2,300 mi.	41,900 ft		7,125/10,100 lb maximum	32'3"/37'
LUFTWAFFE						
BF-109G-6	/386 mph	620 mi.	37,890 ft		5,893/7,491 lb	29'.5"/32'6.5"
BF-110F-2	248-311/352 mph	745 mi.	35,760 ft		12,346/15,873 lb	39'7.25"/53'3.75"
FW-190A-8	298/408 mph	497 mi.	33,800 ft		7,652/10,800 lb	29'4.75"/34'5.5"
FW-190D-9	/426 mph	520 mi.	32,810 ft		7,694/10,670 lb	33'5.25"/34'5.5"
ME-163B-1A	/596 mph	Local	39,500 ft		4,200/9,500 lb	19'2.33"/30'7.33"
ME-262A-1A	/540 mph	652 mi.	37,565 ft		8,378/15,720 lb	34'9.5"/40'11.5"

(Assembling a diverse table of specifications such as this appendix is fraught with pitfalls, ranging from variances noted in different sources to varied methods of computing empty weights [some with and some without equipment on board], plus changes in other attributes. If these numbers represent broad technical baselines, the actuality of combat could skew the performance of any given aircraft depending on weather, altitude, individual aircraft condition, and pilot skill. If trends emerge from this listing, they would seem to show an overwhelming AAF superiority in range with no sacrifice in performance in piston-engine fighters. Statistics for range are particularly difficult to pin down; one formula suggests actual escort range of a given AAF fighter worked out to around 3/8 of its maximum straight-line range; even with long ultimate or ferry range figures posted for P-38s, in practice P-51Ds dominated the skies over Germany. The menace posed by the jet-powered ME-262A is undeniable, but various factors including logistics and availability favored the AAF.)

Red Letter Dates: Eighth Air Force Chronology

The planners, fliers, maintainers, and supporters of the massive Eighth Air Force effort influenced, and were influenced by, the changing war raging around them. The following events capture some of that change and provide context to what the Eighth Air Force's warplanes did.

JANUARY 14, 1942: At the conclusion of the Arcadia conference, the policy of emphasizing the war against Germany while trying initially to contain Japanese offensives suggests a high priority for the forthcoming Eighth Air Force.

JANUARY 28, 1942: Eighth Air Force activated at Savannah, Georgia.

FEBRUARY 1, 1942: Two key elements of Eighth Air Force, VIII Bomber Command and VII Fighter Command, are activated.

FEBRUARY 23, 1942: VIII Bomber Command headquarters established in England under command of General Ira Eaker.

MARCH 25, 1942: Major Cecil P. Lessig becomes first Eighth Air Force pilot to fly a mission over France in the war, operating a Spitfire with Royal Air Force 64 Squadron.

MARCH 31, 1942: General Carl Spaatz suggests the Eighth Air Force be made the nucleus of Army Air Forces in Britain (AAFIB).

APRIL 12, 1942: AAF's plans for aerial component of Operation Bolero, the build-up of forces in the U.K. or attacking German-held Europe, called for the establishment of the Eighth Air Force in England.

MAY 5, 1942: General Carl Spaatz assumes command of Eighth Air Force.

JUNE 8, 1942: Presidential directive establishes European Theater of Operations (ETO).

JUNE 18, 1942: British Air Ministry publishes tentative list of 87 airfields that could be made available to Eighth Air Force.

JUNE 20, 1942: American plans broadly call for the AAF in the ETO to secure air supremacy over Western Europe in anticipation of an invasion of the Continent.

JUNE 23, 1942: Invasion of the European continent is put off (optimistically) until the spring of 1943 to enable resources to be applied to Operation Torch, the invasion of North Africa.

JUNE 29, 1942: First member of Eighth Air Force to drop bombs on enemy-held Europe is Captain Charles C. Kegelman, commander of the 15th Bomb Squadron, who participates in an RAF Douglas Boston attack on Hazebrouck marshaling yard on this date.

JULY 4, 1942: Symbolic date marks the first AAF air operation over Western Europe as six Douglas Boston bombers borrowed from the RAF by the 15th Bomb Squadron join in an RAF low-level attack of four airfields in the Netherlands.

JULY 21, 1942: General Dwight D. Eisenhower assigns Eighth Air Force the mission of attaining air domination over western France by April 1, 1943, in collaboration with the RAF.

JULY 26, 1942: First Eighth Air Force fighter pilot shot down in ETO is Lieutenant Colonel Albert P. Clark of 31st Fighter Group, who becomes a prisoner of war on this date.

AUGUST 1, 1942: Emerging thrust of Eighth Air Force solidifies as General Eaker describes VIII Bomber Command's mission as the destruction of carefully chosen strategic targets in Europe.

AUGUST 5, 1942: VIII Fighter Command launches its first mission when 11 31st Fighter Group aircraft make a practice run over France.

AUGUST 11, 1942: General Spaatz tells General Arnold that it is his opinion only the U.K. can serve as the base from which to achieve air supremacy over Germany, as opposed to any footholds that might be gained from Operation Torch in North Africa.

AUGUST 17, 1942: First Eighth Air Force heavy bomber attack from the U.K. against Western Europe is launched by a dozen B-17s of the 97th Bomb Group, escorted by Spitfires as they attack Rouen-Sotteville marshaling yards. Sergeant Kent R. West becomes first Eighth Air Force bomber gunner to be credited with a combat victory when he shoots down a German fighter during the mission.

This dramatic photo shows late-war 388th Bomb Group B-17Gs flying low with bomb bay doors open. This may have been part of humanitarian food drops conducted over Holland in 1945. Kolln collection

AUGUST 19, 1942: Second Eighth Air Force bombing mission sends 22 B-17s over occupied French airfields at Abbeville/Drucat. Mission is a deliberate attempt to draw German fighters away from a probing coastal invasion by 5,000 Canadian and Allied troops at Dieppe. First Eighth Air Force fighter victory from the U.K. is scored by Second Lieutenant Samuel Junkin, Jr., of 309th Fighter Squadron, whose Spitfire was used to support the Dieppe raid.

AUGUST 21, 1942: A mission to bomb shipyards at Rotterdam is called back while under attack by 25 Luftwaffe fighters. Since the bombers cannot capitalize on Spitfire escort, due in part to lack of proper coordination, recall is ordered from headquarters in England.

SEPTEMBER 6, 1942: First VIII Bomber Command combat losses occur when fighters down two B-17s over Meaulte, France.

SEPTEMBER 8, 1942: Joint British American Directive on Day Bomber Operations Involving Fighter Cooperation, an effort of the RAF and Eighth Air Force, formally delineates day bombing to the Eighth Air Force and night bombing to the RAF.

SEPTEMBER 9, 1942: Even as Eighth Air Force is drained by requirements to support creation of Twelfth Air Force for Operation Torch, a plan devised to replenish the Eighth is submitted by General Arnold to the Chief of Staff.

SEPTEMBER 29, 1942: American fighter pilots who had flown in three Royal Air Force Eagle Squadrons are taken into VIII Fighter Command and established as the 4th Fighter group.

OCTOBER 9, 1942: Consolidated B-24D Liberators join Eighth Air Force bomber operations in a combined effort with B-17s that marks the first American mission from the U.K. to launch more than 100 bombers.

OCTOBER 20, 1942: Despite AAF efforts to create a strategic role for the Eighth Air Force with great autonomy from ground support roles dictated by the Army, on this date General Eisenhower issues a directive supporting Operation Torch by requiring Eighth Air Force to give first priority to the protection of men and supplies moving from the U.K. to North Africa, by attacking German submarine bases on the west coast of France.

NOVEMBER 9, 1942: When previous high-altitude missions have disappointing results against German submarine pens, VIII Bomber Command attacks the U-boat base at Saint-Nazaire with a dozen B-24Ds at 17,500 to 18,300 feet and 31 B-17s at lower altitudes ranging from 7,500 to 10,000 feet. The higher B-24 Liberators report little antiaircraft damage, but the low-flying B-17 Fortresses have 22 aircraft damaged by AA fire and three downed. There will be no more low-level heavy bomber missions against submarine bases.

NOVEMBER 23, 1942: During high-altitude attack on submarine base at Saint-Nazaire, Eighth Air Force bomber crews note a change in Luftwaffe fighter tactics. German fighters switch from tail attacks to head-on passes to take advantage of the weaker frontal firepower of early B-17s and B-24s. This will lead to the development of versions of both bombers with power nose or chin turrets.

NOVEMBER 30, 1942: Agreement between British and Americans assigns responsibility for air defense of American airfields in England to the RAF, acknowledging VIII Fighter Command's primary role as escorts for bombers on missions over the Continent.

JANUARY 3, 1943: A 68-bomber attack on the Saint-Nazaire submarine base is the heaviest to date against a sub base. For the first time in VIII Bomber Command, the aircraft employ formation precision bombing instead of individual bombing, recording considerable damage on the dock area. The Germans, too, are evolving tactics as they use an effective pre-directed flak barrage instead of trying to track the bombers. Seven aircraft are lost and 47 are damaged.

JANUARY 27, 1943: First Eighth Air Force attack on Germany sees 53 heavy bombers strike various harbor-related targets in Wilhelmshaven while 2 more heavy bombers hit the submarine base at Emden.

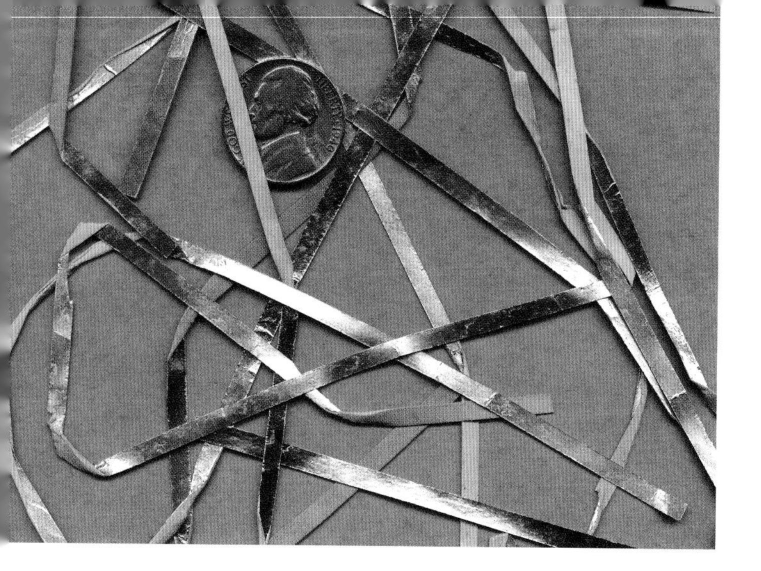

A Jefferson nickel coin provides size comparison for strips of foil/paper chaff that was used by Eighth Air Force bombers to obscure German antiaircraft radar images. Dave and Jeff Sturges, via Don Keller

Newly introduced Sperry lower ball turret was photographed on a B-17E at Boeing's Seattle plant in February 1942. This turret rectified deficiencies of earlier ventral B-17 armaments. Boeing photo

MARCH 4, 1943: First Eighth Air Force attack on an industrial target in the Ruhr takes place as 16 heavy bombers strike the marshaling yards at Hamm.

MARCH 18, 1943: Eighth Air Force achieves first successful combat use of automatic flight control linked to bombsights during a 97-bomber attack on submarine yards at Vegesack, Germany. Reports indicate substantial damage has been inflicted on seven U-boat hulls.

APRIL 12, 1943: Five Eighth Air Force officers and one Royal Air Force counterpart finish drafting the plan for the Combined Bomber Offensive (CBO) to be conducted from the United Kingdom.

APRIL 17, 1943: Eighth Air Force's largest mission to date sends 106 heavy bombers against the Focke Wulf factory at Bremen. Aggressive fighters claim 15 bombers as flak downs the 16th loss that day. VIII Fighter Command calls for 20 fighter groups to thwart the increasing threat German fighters pose to the Combined Bomber Offensive.

MAY 4, 1943: Eighth Air Force P-47s begin escorting bombers as deep as 175 miles.

MAY 17, 1943: An early Eighth Air Force low-level attack by twin-engine B-26 Marauders of the 322nd Bomb Group results in the loss of 10 of 11 B-26s on the raid against power stations at Ijmuiden and Haarlem in the Netherlands. Eighth Air Force stops low-level medium bomber attacks following this loss.

MAY 18, 1943: U.S./British Combined Chiefs of Staff (CCS) approve Combined Bomber Offensive (CBO) plan for round-the-clock attacks on German targets by Eighth Air Force and RAF. This adds credence to Eighth Air Force's long-standing beliefs on how the war should be prosecuted. Eighth Air Force will concentrate on precision daylight bombing while RAF is to bomb strategic city areas by night. Target priority list begins with destruction of Luftwaffe fighters, followed in order by German submarine yards and bases, German aircraft industry, ball bearing plants, and oil industry (especially from planned attacks against the captured oilfields at Ploesti, Romania). Secondary objectives include synthetic rubber and tires and military motor transportation. Contingencies will intrude on this list before war's end.

MAY 29, 1943: Combat debut of YB-40 gunnery escort versions of the B-17F, joining Eighth Air Force B-17s on a mission to locks and sub pens at Saint-Nazaire.

JUNE 30, 1943: VIII Fighter Command becomes independent of Royal Air Force operational control, with Eighth Air Force's fighter assets now under the control of the 65th Fighter Wing.

JULY 1, 1943: Memo to General Arnold from General Giles says current ratio of one fighter group to four heavy bomber groups is insufficient; recommends minimum ratio be one to two.

JULY 22, 1943: British report on early Combined Bomber Offensive (CBO) activity reveals a mixed blessing as Luftwaffe fighter assets in the Mediterranean and Eastern fronts have been diluted so more than half of Germany's fighter strength can be employed defensively over Western Europe to challenge Eighth Air Force.

JULY 24, 1943: A new assembly procedure is introduced for when inclement weather over England prevents climbing in formation. The new method launches bombers individually on instruments, en route to a designated radio "splasher beacon" for bomb group assembly, and thence to three more splasher beacons to coalesce the entire bombing force. This development enables many missions to proceed that would otherwise be doomed by bad weather. Eighth Air Force sends 167 heavy bombers against German-held mineral plants and naval sites in Norway following the successful join-up via splasher beacons this day.

AUGUST 17, 1943: First anniversary of Eighth Air Force heavy bomber operations is observed by launching 315 bombers on the deepest penetration of Germany to date, striking a Messerschmitt aircraft plant at Regensburg and bearing factories at Schweinfurt. Staggering loss of 60 B-17s is a setback that cannot be sustained routinely by Eighth Air Force.

AUGUST 30, 1943: Radar-equipped 482nd Bomb Group becomes operational; will use its pathfinder B-17s and B-24s sprinkled among other groups to find targets in Germany through overcast conditions. Later, bomb groups will have their own radar-equipped pathfinders.

Four ordnance crew members use steel bars hooked into bomb shackles to heft a 500-pound bomb for loading in a 388th Bomb Group B-17 on August 20, 1943. The large hexagon-head bolt in the bomb's nose will be replaced with a fuse that will arm the falling bomb in flight as the slipstream spins a small propeller. AAF

Ruby Newall was a WAC who was selected to be immortalized on a B-17, and the 385th Bomb Group saw to it that she was properly portrayed. USAFA/Brown

SEPTEMBER 6, 1943: Eighth Air Force dispatches a record 407 heavy bombers, 69 of which are supposed to fly a diversion. Weather fouls some target plans, but 262 heavy bombers ultimately strike targets of opportunity in France and Germany.

SEPTEMBER 27, 1943: Two milestones are reached this day: Relying on a pair of H2S radar-equipped pathfinder bombers, 244 B-17s fly the first large-scale daylight mission in the ETO above an overcast target, the German port of Emden. And this is the first bomber mission escorted all the way to a German target by P-47s. Generally, radar bombing through overcast will be restricted to targets within Germany.

OCTOBER 8, 1943: First use by Eighth Air Force of Carpet jamming transmitters to confound German radar; this occurs during a mission to Bremen.

OCTOBER 14, 1943: Another withering loss of 60 B-17s, plus others written off in England, by Eighth Air Force in attack on Schweinfurt causes a temporary discontinuance of daylight bombing against strategic targets deep in Germany. The loss rate this day more than doubles the 10 percent that Eighth Air Force considers prohibitive.

Uncensored tabs on these two photos show the results of Eighth Air Force bombing of specific targets in occupied Brussels and Paris. Targeting occupied countries could be a delicate matter, and the AAF tried to minimize the loss of life to civilians. In many cases, the use of the evolving technique of radar bombing was limited to targets within Germany, where concerns about collateral damage were less elevated. AAF

NOVEMBER 3, 1943: New Eighth Air Force record of 539 B-17s and B-24s, including 11 radar-equipped pathfinders, do substantial damage to the German port of Wilhelmshaven. P-38s get their first serious taste of combat over Western Europe, claiming three Luftwaffe airplanes downed as the P-38s escort the bombers most of the distance to the target.

DECEMBER 3, 1943: The Combined Bomber Offensive against the German Air Force is assessed by some to be three months behind schedule for anticipated invasion of Western Europe. This results in more pressure on Eighth Air Force to target industries vital to warplane production.

DECEMBER 20, 1943: First Eighth Air Force use of Window (metal foil strips which obscure accurate German radar images) occurs during strike against Bremen.

DECEMBER 24, 1943: With 26 heavy bomber groups available for combat, Eighth Air Force's largest mission to date sends 670 B-17s and B-24s against 23 V-weapon launch sites in the Pas de Calais region of France. This marks the first major Eighth Air Force strike against the launch sites.

DECEMBER 31, 1943: Bomb tonnage dropped by Eighth Air Force this month (13,142 tons) exceeds that of Royal Air Force Bomber Command for the first time.

JANUARY 1, 1944: United States Strategic Air Forces in Europe (USSAFE, later USSTAF) is established for operational control of Eighth and Fifteenth Air Forces.

JANUARY 5, 1944: An Eighth Air Force report says U.S. daylight strategic bombardment campaign against Germany will be endangered unless steps are taken to reduce German fighter strength. German fighter gains have been made through increased production, improved firepower, and allocation of more fighters to the Western Front.

JANUARY 24, 1944: Americans and British in England agree to put most of the available P-51 Mustangs in Eighth Air Force for long-range escort duty. Ultimately, Eighth Air Force will winnow out many of its P-47s and P-38s in favor of P-51s.

FEBRUARY 11, 1944: First P-51 Mustangs come to VIII Fighter Command.

MARCH 4, 1944: Thirty-one B-17s are first U.S. bombers to attack the Berlin area when they bomb the Kleinmachnow area southwest of the city.

MARCH 6, 1944: Eighth Air Force returns to Berlin in force, with 658 heavy bombers attacking the metropolitan area as well as targets of opportunity in nearby cities. Highest one-day loss to date is incurred when aggressive fighter opposition downs 69 American bombers. The presence of escorting P-38s and especially P-51s over the German capital city foretells the winning combination that would sustain Eighth Air Force heavy bomber operations deep inside Germany.

APRIL 11, 1944: Three forces totaling 830 B-24s and B-17s bombs fighter aircraft production plants and other targets in Germany, suffering the loss of 64 bombers to enemy action. During this period, attacks on German aircraft production and airfields receive repeated attention in an urgent effort to blunt the Luftwaffe's growing capabilities in the West.

MAY 7, 1944: Hundreds of B-17s and B-24s attacked a variety of targets in the morning and afternoon, marking the first time that more than 900 Eighth Air Force heavy bombers strike targets in a day and the first time more than 1,000 are airborne on a single day's operations.

MAY 9, 1944: Starting this date, airfield attacks within a month before the planned D-Day invasion take on new

B-17 aircrew members attend a briefing during the shuttle bombing of German targets, which involved temporary use of Soviet airfields in an edgy alliance. USAFA/Brown

German bombers raided Poltava in the middle of the night on June 21, 1944, destroying 47 B-17s and about a dozen P-51s parked on the Soviet airfield for a shuttle-bombing mission. USAFA/Brown

importance as Allied planners seek to disable Luftwaffe fields and take them out of service. A total of 797 B-24s and B-17s inaugurates this offensive over 9 French fields, as well as several marshaling yards.

MAY 22, 1944: Eighth Air Force completes occupancy of all planned stations in England, including 66 airfields.

MAY 26, 1944: Eighth Air Force reaches peak fighter group strength when the P-38-equipped 479th Fighter Group becomes operational. By year's end, all but one of the Eighth Air Force fighter groups will fly P-51s.

JUNE 2–5, 1944: Eighth Air Force heavy bombers participate in Operation Cover, a feint of attacks in the Pas de Calais area to make the Germans believe any impending invasion would take place there instead of the real location, Normandy.

JUNE 6, 1944: Top strength of Eighth Air Force is realized when the 493rd Bomb Group's initial complement of B-24s becomes operational, making a total of 40 heavy bomb groups. The first Normandy invasion support mission of the day sees 1,361 heavy bombers of the Eighth dispatched, with more than 1,000 of them sent to attack beach installations. By day's end, 1,729 Eighth Air Force heavy bomber sorties have dropped 3,596 tons of bombs, with the loss of only three bombers (caused by a collision and ground fire).

JUNE 8, 1944: Encouraged by the results of attacks on German oil targets in May, General Spaatz places oil in the first priority of targets for USSTAF missions.

JUNE 21, 1944: First Eighth Air Force shuttle bombing mission sees 144 B-17s land at Poltava and Mirgorod in the Soviet Union after bombing targets including a synthetic oil plant at Ruhland. A cache of fuel and munitions awaits the bombers at their Russian airfields for a return strike on the way to the AAF facility at Foggia, Italy. That night, German bombers destroy 47 B-17s on the ground in Russia and damage more.

JULY 20, 1944: The growing might of the Eighth Air Force juggernaut is exemplified by more than 1,200 heavy bombers striking numerous targets in central Germany, with an escort totaling 727 fighters—numbers that had to be vexing to German defenders.

AUGUST 28, 1944: When weather keeps Eighth Air Force's heavy bombers from operating this day, eight P-51 fighter groups go on strafing sweeps over Western Europe. At day's end, the Mustang fliers claim 8 enemy aircraft and almost 150 locomotives destroyed, at a price of 16 P-51s.

SEPTEMBER 1944: This month some of Eighth Air Force's big, versatile B-24s are detailed to haul supplies and gasoline into France, even as other Eighth Air Force heavy bombers are groomed to destroy Axis petroleum capacity.

SEPTEMBER 27, 1944: Almost 1,100 heavy bombers rise from England and attack several targets in Germany, including two synthetic oil plants as Eighth Air Force strength continues to grow.

NOVEMBER 8, 1944: A sign that the war is progressing toward an Allied victory comes when the VIII Air Force Composite Command ceases operations as its personnel are attached to the provisional Air Disarmament Command by USSTAF. Also on this date Eighth Air Force is assigned its first airfield on the Continent, at Denain/Prouvy, as a step toward enabling the Eighth to service its aircraft in the area. Even though heavy bomber operations continue to operate from bases in England, the presence of Allied-held airfields on the Continent affords damaged Eighth Air Force aircraft more safe havens.

DECEMBER 24, 1944: Christmas Eve sees more than 2,000 Eighth Air Force heavy bombers dispatched (with nearly 1,900 of them actually making attacks) against a wide array of targets in battle areas.

JANUARY 18, 1945: After bombing the marshaling yards at Kaiserslautern, the majority of the 100-plus B-17s on the mission divert to land at bases on the Continent because of weather.

JANUARY 23, 1945: An Eighth Air Force P-51 Mustang fighter group, now based on the Continent to take advantage of Allied holdings, launches a fighter sweep.

MARCH 19, 1945: Even as Eighth Air Force continues its momentum over Germany, a noteworthy count of 36 Luftwaffe jet fighters in formation, the largest grouping encountered to date, is reported. Escorting P-51s claim three of the jets downed, along with 39 piston-engine German fighters.

MARCH 21, 1945: A respite from typical ongoing missions against synthetic petroleum plants and transportation hubs comes as Eighth Air Force heavy bombers are tasked for several days of bombing in support of the impending Allied armies' crossing of the lower Rhine River. Targets for several days will include German airfields, marshaling yards, and troop concentrations. By March 24, a force of 235 Eighth Air Force B-24 Liberators is used to airdrop supplies to Allied forces east of the Rhine.

APRIL 7, 1945: Fighters escorting Eighth Air Force bombers count more than 50 German jet fighters among the Luftwaffe opposition. Two days later, 10 German jet airfields are among the targets of the Eighth Air Force.

APRIL 15, 1945: Eighth Air Force's only operational use of napalm, delivered against German defensive ground installations at Royan, France, by almost 850 heavy bombers, gives disappointing results.

APRIL 25, 1945: Under escort by four P-51 groups, about 275 B-17s conduct Eighth Air Force's final heavy bomber mission of the war against an industrial target when they bomb an armament works and airfield in German-held Czechoslovakia. A similar number of Eighth Air Force B-24s bombs marshaling yards and a transformer station elsewhere over Europe.

APRIL 27, 1945: With victory near, the influx of replacement B-24s, B-17s, and P-51s to Eighth Air Force has stopped by this date. Enlarged authorizations of 68 bombers and 96 fighters per group have been scaled back to original figures of 48 bombers and 75 fighters.

MAY 1, 1945: Eighth Air Force B-17s begin several days of sorties dropping food to the civilian population in parts of the Netherlands where flooding and combat have led to serious shortages.

MAY 7, 1945: Germany surrenders unconditionally, effective May 9.

MAY 9, 1945: First Eighth Air Force bomb group to be redeployed after cessation of hostilities, the Liberator-equipped 453rd begins leaving Old Buckenham on this date without its aircraft.

(See also Kit C. Carter and Robert Mueller, compilers, *Combat Chronology 1941–1945: U.S. Army Air Forces in World War II*, Center for Air Force History, Washington, D.C., 1991; *Eighth Air Force Story*, Kenn C. Rust, Historical Aviation Album, Temple City, Calif., 1978.)

On February 25, 1945, 486th Bomb Group B-17Gs cruise over a European countryside that appears both forested and logged. The Fortress in the center of the photo uses the enclosed radio room gun hatch with a K-6 gun mount. Brilliant yellow tail markings, Square-W logos, and chevrons or color slashes on wings established the unit's identity to the initiated, similar to the arcane signals from a baseball team manager to a pitcher during a heated game. AAF

Index

WAR in PACIFIC SKIES

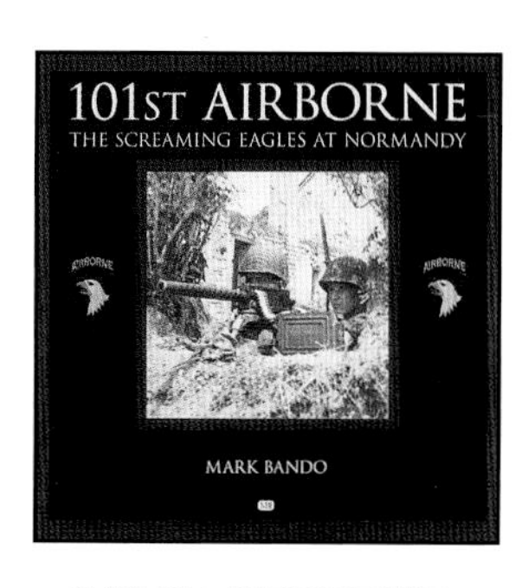
101ST AIRBORNE
THE SCREAMING EAGLES AT NORMANDY
MARK BANDO

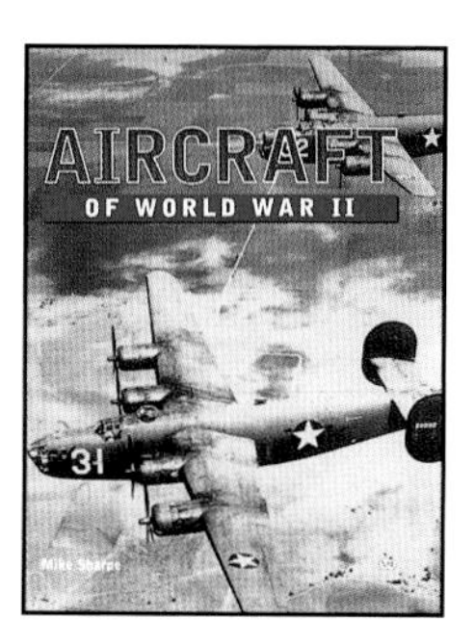
AIRCRAFT
OF WORLD WAR II

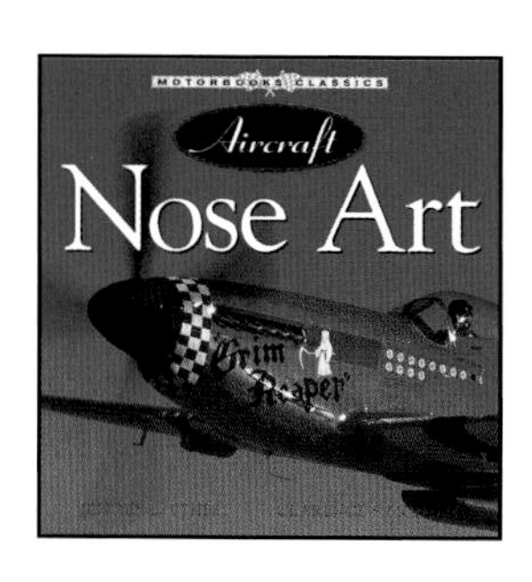
Aircraft
Nose Art

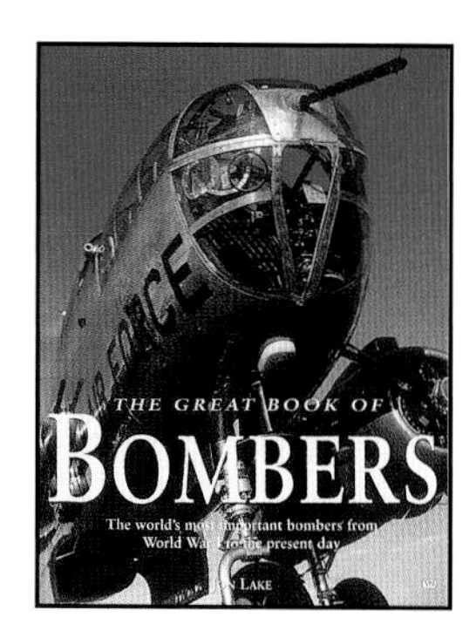
THE GREAT BOOK OF
BOMBERS

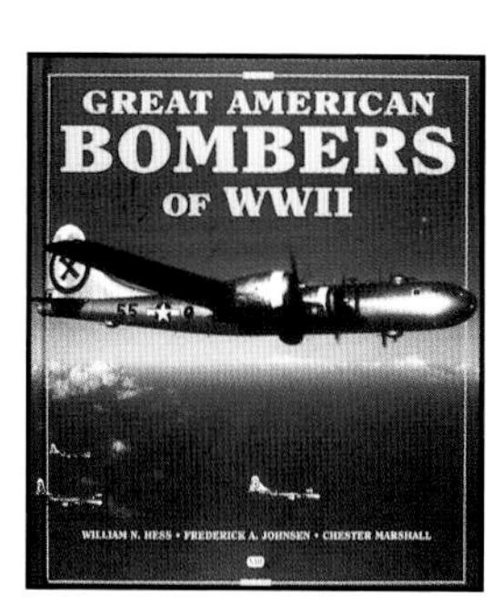
GREAT AMERICAN
BOMBERS
OF WWII

GUN CAMERA
- WORLD WAR II
L. DOUGLAS KEENEY

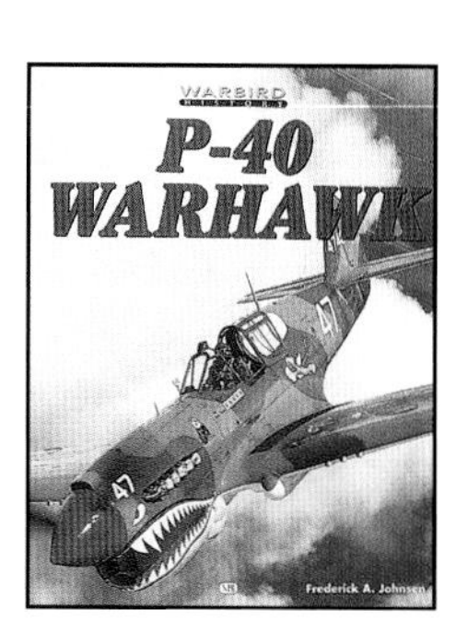
P-40
WARHAWK
Frederick A. Johnsen

WORLD WAR II
Day by Day
Antony Shaw